CONTENTS

Ships in Focus Publications
Correspondence and editorial:
Roy Fenton
18 Durrington Avenue
London SW20 8NT
020 8879 3527
rfenton@rfenton.demon.co.uk
Orders and photographic:
John & Marion Clarkson
18 Franklands, Longton
Preston PR4 5PD
01772 612855
shipsinfocus@btinternet.com

Printed by Amadeus Press Ltd., Cleckheaton,
Yorkshire.
Designed by Hugh Smallwood, John
Clarkson and Roy Fenton.

SHIPS IN FOCUS RECORD
ISBN 1 901703 78 9

SHIPS IN FOCUS RECORD 32
November 2005

This issue includes the concluding part of Malcolm Cooper's examination of Aitken, Milburn's Loch Line, its fortunes and especially its misfortunes, which began in *Record* 30. This part, a fleet list with many further photographs, should have appeared in *Record* 31, but as some of the photographs needed to illustrate it were delayed, the decision was made late in the production process to substitute another article. As our readers know, we like to include a photograph of every ship we feature if at all possible, but sometimes circumstances outside our control conspire to delay us.

In contrast, the omission of credits from the short article on the old steamer *Spidola* in *Record* 31 was not deliberate, but was due to an editor's forgetfulness. It should have been made clear that a major source for the narrative was Dr David Jenkin's 'Owen and Watkin Williams of Cardiff: The Golden Cross Line' (World Ship Society, Kendal, 1991). This was especially naughty because *Record* 31 included an article by David. Profuse apologies.

Quoting sources of information and acknowledging those whose material is cited is something we consider important, and all our authors are encouraged to provide such information, unless their sources are clear from the text of their article, as in the case of Ken Garrett's 'The donkeyman's tale' in this issue. One exception is short captions to photographs, where such acknowledgements could easily be longer than the text.

In our quest for more subscribers to *Record*, we are offering to all who take out a subscription the possibility of buying back numbers of *Record* at just £3.50 each. This facility is, naturally, open to all subscribers. The advantages of a subscription include each issue arriving as soon as it is published, a reduction in price compared with ordering each issue separately, and offers on other Ships in Focus books. Of course, the subscription is an advantage to the publisher, as it helps determine the print run, and assures us we will sell a minimum number. So, if you do not already subscribe, please consider doing so. And if you do, apply for your half-price back issues, and encourage others to subscribe. If new subscribers tell us they were introduced by you, we'll send you a small, shipping-related present!

Subscribers will also find enclosed with this issue a further small 'thank you' item.

John Clarkson   Roy Fenton
November 2005

SUBSCRIPTION RATES FOR RECORD

Readers may start their subscription with any issue, and are welcome to backdate it to receive any previous issues.

	3 issues	4 issues
UK	£23	£31
Europe (airmail)	£25	£34
Rest of world (surface)	£25	£34
Rest of world (airmail)	£30	£40

GW00707439

Victoria Dock, Melbourne on 3rd January 1908 when seven Loch Line vessels were berthed. Left to right, they were: *Loch Etive, Loch Broom, Loch Garry, Loch Katrine, Loch Carron, Loch Tay* and *Loch Torridon*. [Melbourne Harbour Trust Commissioners; author's collection]

Jersey City of 1882 in the Avon Gorge approaching Bristol. *[York Collection/World Ship Society Ltd.]*

Wells City (2) of 1890. *[World Ship Society Ltd.]*

Fleet in Focus

BRISTOL CITY LINE - Part 1
Geoffrey Holmes

When he planned the Great Western Railway, Brunel's vision was for a through service by rail and steamship from London via Bristol to North America, the Orient, Australia and New Zealand. Such an integrated service was not, in fact, achieved until Canadian Pacific established their express service from Liverpool in 1906. Although *Great Western* originally sailed from Bristol she was transferred to Liverpool in 1846 and it was to be a further 25 years before a regular service across the Atlantic was again based in Bristol.

In 1828 Mark Whitwell had sailed as master in vessels belonging to James Hillhouse and in 1871 he established the Great Western Steamship Line with the steamer *Arragon*. Over the next 10 years the fleet expanded and by 1879 the company had six ships in service.

The works to divert the River Avon and enclose the river's old course to form the Great Floating Harbour were completed in 1809. However, the cost of construction was well above budget and, as a result, the Bristol Dock Company set very high dues causing traffic to use other more competitive ports.

When construction of *Great Britain* was planned in1839 the owners had, as they thought, come to an agreement with the Bristol Dock Company for the locks into the Cumberland Basin (44 feet) and from there to the river (45 feet) to be widened to accommodate the ship's 50-foot beam. In the event this widening had not been done and in October 1844, after Brunel had employed labourers with picks and shovels to give sufficient width, the ship passed through to the Cumberland Basin and on into the river in December. The locks were afterwards restored to their original dimensions and it was not until about 1870 that the entrances were widened to 62 feet.

Charles Hill and Sons.

James Hillhouse had become established as a merchant in Bristol in the early eighteenth century. The family became prosperous through privateering. James Hillhouse's grandson, James Martin Hillhouse, established a shipbuilding yard on the north bank of the Avon at Hotwells and in 1810 Charles Hill entered his employment becoming a partner in the business fifteen years later. In 1840 the name of the firm was changed to Hillhouse and Hill and when, in 1845, Charles Hill took full control it became Charles Hill and Sons.

By this time the original yard at Hotwells and another yard nearer to Bristol city centre had been abandoned and the company's shipbuilding activities were concentrated at the Albion Dockyard on the south side of the harbour (next to Pattersons yard where *Great Britain* was built). Hills continued building ships on this site until 1976. The company also continued as ship owners and in 1877 was prospering, owning 19 sailing ships.

The Bristol City Line: the early years

In 1878 Charles Hill's grandsons, Charles Gathorne Hill and Edward Burrow Hill, entered the firm. Gathorne persuaded his father - Charles Hill (junior) - and Uncle - Edward Stock Hill that the time was ripe to start a steamship line from Bristol to New York. Avonmouth Dock had been opened in 1877 and Mark Whitwell's Great Western Steamship Line had moved downstream to the new dock. However, it was decided that, as access to Avonmouth from Bristol was poor, the ships would trade from the City Docks. This was in spite of the existence of the railway from Hotwells to Avonmouth along the Avon Gorge (opened in 1865 this was replaced by the Portway road in 1926). The wisdom of the policy of sailing from Bristol was to be shown in 1895 when Mark Whitwell was forced to wind up his company through lack of trade.

Orders were placed with Richardson, Duck and Co. for two ships: *Bristol City* and *New York City*. These were of modest size and, unlike Whitwell's ships, did not carry passengers. They proved to be such an immediate success that a third ship, *Bath City*, was quickly ordered commencing her maiden voyage only seven months after *Bristol City*. A fourth steamer, *Brooklyn City*, was ordered and entered service in March 1881. However, this year proved to be disastrous for the fledgling company as *Bristol City* disappeared after leaving New York on 28th December 1880 and *Bath City* sprang a leak and foundered off the Grand Banks on 3rd December 1881. *Gloucester City* was delivered at the end of the year to be followed by *Jersey City* and *Llandaff City* during 1882. These three ships were an improvement on the earlier design. *Gloucester City* was to have only a short career, being lost after colliding with ice floes in February 1883.

Wells City was delivered in November 1885, the company's first steel ship. She too was only destined for a short career: arriving in New York in February 1887 and about to anchor she was struck by ice floating down the Hudson. This swept her on to a coastal steamer *Lone Star* causing severe damage resulting in *Wells City* sinking after 20 minutes, fortunately without loss of life.

In 1890 the Albion Dockyard delivered the second *Wells City*, the first vessel to be built for the company by their own yard. Her entry into service brought the fleet up to six. *Wells City* (2) was to serve the company for 37 years.

At the end of the century there were ten ships in service and the line was now able to despatch a ship to New York every four days. However, this was not to last. On 14th February 1900 the new *Bath City* (2) was homeward bound from her fourth voyage when she was wrecked on Lundy Island. Ironically, the captain, being unsure of his position, had turned back through fear of grounding on Lundy. This highlights the problems of dead reckoning navigation before electronic aids became available. Another casualty in the early years of the twentieth century was *Boston City*, which sank after a collision in New York harbour in 1904.

Salvage, broken shafts and accidents

During the company's first 25 years its steamers were involved in numerous salvage operations. *Bristol City* (1) had, on her last westbound voyage, towed a derelict barque into Queenstown and, nearing New York, had picked up the crew of a US schooner. However, it was Captain Weiss who became a legend on the North Atlantic for his skill at finding vessels needing assistance and his seamanship in towing them safely to port. In seven years whilst in command of first *Brooklyn City* (1) and later *Wells City* (1) he towed five vessels in to port and rescued the crews of a further two - Cunard's *Palmyra* and Wilson's *Albano* being amongst the ships assisted. The normal reason for steamers seeking assistance was a broken propeller or tail shaft or a lost rudder. Bristol City Line's ships were not immune to this problem as both *Jersey City* and *Llandaff City* were towed in (1891 and 1892 respectively). The following year *Llandaff City* towed the Anchor liner *Olympia* into Halifax.

The most notable salvage operation performed by the company's ships was when *Kansas City* towed the White Star *Cufic* into Queenstown in December 1900. This operation took ten days in very bad weather. Again the problem was a broken tail shaft. Improvement in casting techniques and, as the size of ships increased, more twin-screw ships meant that such incidents became less common. *Boston City* towed the Russian steamer *Erika* to a safe anchorage off Newport in February 1903.

From 1891 the second *Gloucester City* is listed in Lloyd's Register as being owned by W.R. Corfield Ltd. However, she appears to have remained a unit of the Bristol City Line fleet. In his 'Ship Shape and Bristol Fashion' John C.G. Hill relates how two of Hill's sailing ships - both named *Avonmore* - were wrecked. The first had sailed from Cardiff for Montevideo in September 1869 and when 30 miles west of the Scilly Isles encountered hurricane strength winds that forced her back along the north Cornish coast until she was

blown ashore near Bude. The master, W.R. Corfield, was one of the survivors of this wreck.

In May 1877 the company's second *Avonmore* was one of some 30 ships anchored off Huanillos, Peru, loading guano. At 8.15 pm on the evening of 9th May the town suffered a major earthquake and the ensuing tsunami tore the ships from their moorings. One was thrown against *Avonmore* causing her to capsize. The crew were washed overboard and Captain Corfield's wife, two children and their nurse were among those lost. Another ship belonging to Hills, *Conference,* was thrown ashore and wrecked. It appears that after this tragedy Captain Corfield formed a company that was associated with Hills. The unfortunate Captain holds what must be a uniquely tragic and unenviable record.

The start of the 20th century

The completion of *New York City* (2) in 1907 brought the fleet back up to nine. However trade was very bad and, as a result, in 1909 the three oldest ships were laid up in Swansea and subsequently sold. It is interesting to compare *New York City* (2) with contemporary ships of other cargo-only companies on the North Atlantic. For instance, in 1904 Manchester Liners commissioned three ships. These were 50 feet longer and 6 feet more in the beam, drawing 6 feet more. The obvious conclusion from this comparison is that the Bristol ships were constrained by the limitations of Bristol Docks and the River Avon. However, by 1907, the Royal Edward Dock was open at Avonmouth and this could accommodate virtually any ship then in service. It is thought that the real reason for the company's small ship policy was that the Bristol Channel ports could not generate sufficient freight westbound to justify larger ships. Although Cardiff was, at that time, Britain's biggest export port; its trade was almost all coal and steel. Swansea and Newport were also virtually dependent on these two commodities, both, of course, abundant in the USA.

Although Bristol had good rail links to London, Birmingham and the Black Country, its industrial hinterland could not match that of Liverpool or Manchester. In John

The launch of *New York City (3)* from the Albion Dockyard, Bristol in 1917. *[Peter Newall collection]*

196

C.G. Hill's book there are several references to Bristol City Line ships loading at two or three Bristol Channel ports or taking cargoes of china clay from Fowey on westbound passages. It was 1919 before the company appointed agents in Birmingham in an attempt to attract traffic from the Midlands.

At the outbreak of the First World War the company was operating six ships. Three of these were lost, two due to enemy action (*New York City* (2) and *Bristol City* (2)) and one through going missing (*Kansas City*). *Boston City* (2) and *New York City* (3) were completed at the Albion Dockyard in 1917 as replacements for lost tonnage, but when only 11 months old the former became the company's fourth war loss. In contrast, *New York City* (3) was destined to serve the company for 33 years. A total of 62 lives were lost on Bristol City Line ships during the war.

Fleet list

1. BRISTOL CITY (1) 1879-1880 Iron
O.N. 78460 1,725g 1,134n 260.0 x 34.5 x 22.5 feet.
C. 2-cyl. (33 and 61 x 33 inches) by Thomas Richardson and Sons, Hartlepool.
7.1879: Launched by Richardson, Duck and Co., Stockton-on-Tees (Yard No. 254) for Charles Hill and Sons, Bristol as BRISTOL CITY.
28.12.1880: Sailed from New York for Bristol and disappeared.

2. NEW YORK CITY (1) 1879-1885 Iron
O.N. 78461 725g 1,131n 260.0 x 34.5 x 22.5 feet.
C. 2-cyl. (33 and 61 x 33 inches) by Thomas Richardson and Sons, Hartlepool.
8.1879: Launched by Richardson, Duck and Co., Stockton-on-Tees (Yard No. 255) for Charles Hill and Sons, Bristol as NEW YORK CITY.
1885: Sold to the New York City Steam Ship Co. Ltd. (Scrutton, Sons and Co., managers), London.
1896: Sold to Navigation à Vapeur Egée (P.M. Courtgi and Co., managers), Constantinople, Turkey and renamed BRAILA.
1912: Sold to M. Rigo, France and renamed ATHINA.
1914: Sold to A. Yannoulatos, Piraeus, Greece.
1917: Sold to Navigation à Vapeur Ionienne (G. Yannoulatos Frères), Piraeus.
4.5.1917: Wrecked near Espozende, Portugal whilst on a voyage from Newport to Algiers with a cargo of coal.

3. BATH CITY (1) 1880-1881 Iron
O.N. 78462 1,725g 1,122n 260.0 x 34.5 x 22.5 feet.
C. 2-cyl. (33 and 61 x 33 inches) by Thomas Richardson and Sons, Hartlepool.
4.1880: Launched by Richardson, Duck and Co., Stockton-on-Tees (Yard No. 256) for Charles Hill and Sons, Bristol as BATH CITY.
12.11.1881: Began to leak in bad weather whilst on a voyage from Bristol for New York with general cargo.
29.11.1881: Captain Ivey ordered 11,000 boxes of tin to be jettisoned. By this time the vessel was in great distress as her rudder had carried away. 180 miles south east of St. John's, Newfoundland, in position 46 north by 45 west, she sighted the steamer MARATHON (2,403/1860) on passage from Liverpool to New York. The BATH CITY requested towing to Halifax but this was refused as the MARATHON did not have sufficient coal.
3.12.1881: Crew abandoned the BATH CITY off the Grand Banks and she was seen to founder about 90 minutes later.
6.12.1881: 21 of the crew were picked up the barque M.J. FOLEY (449/1878). The master and one other man died during the passage to Liverpool. Many of the 19 survivors lost limbs due to exposure.

4. BROOKLYN CITY 1881-1910 Iron
O.N. 78467 1,725g 1,122n 260.0 x 34.5 x 22.5 feet.
C. 2-cyl. (33 and 61 x 33 inches) by Thomas Richardson and Sons, Hartlepool.
2.1881: Launched by Richardson, Duck and Co., Stockton-on-Tees (Yard No.271) for Charles Hill and Sons, Bristol as BROOKLYN CITY.
1909: Laid up at Swansea.
1910: Sold to Compagnia Marittima Siciliano, Milazzo, Sicily, Italy and renamed GIBILTERRA.
27.3.1912: Beached at Derna, Libya following a collision during a voyage from Naples to Derna with a cargo of firewood.
29.5.1912: Refloated and subsequently towed to Torre Annunziata, Italy for breaking up.

5. GLOUCESTER CITY (1) 1881-1883 Iron
O.N. 85802 1,940g 1,268n 270.2 x 36.0 x 23.5 feet.
C. 2-cyl. (36 and 67 x 36 inches) by Thomas Richardson and Sons, Hartlepool.
10.1881: Launched by Richardson, Duck and Co., Stockton-on-Tees (Yard No.281) for Charles Hill and Sons, Bristol as GLOUCESTER CITY.
21.2.1883: Collided with ice flows in position 46.04 north by 47.28 west whilst on passage from Bristol to New York with general cargo.
23.2.1883: Abandoned. The crew were picked up by Danish steamer FERGIA and landed at Le Havre.

6. JERSEY CITY 1882-1910 Iron
O.N. 85803 1,940g 1,261n 270.2 x 36.0 x 23.5 feet.
C. 2-cyl. (36 and 67 x 36 inches) by Thomas Richardson and Sons, Hartlepool.
1882: Launched by Richardson, Duck and Co., Stockton-on-Tees (Yard No.285) for Charles Hill and Sons, Bristol as JERSEY CITY.
1909: Laid up at Swansea.
1910: Sold to Compagnia Marittima Siciliano, Messina, Sicily and renamed BOSFORO.
1912: Sold to African and Eastern Steamship Co. Ltd. (Glynn and Co., managers), Liverpool and renamed SOTERO.
1924: Sold to Schweitzer and Oppler, Berlin, Germany for demolition.

Jersey City (1). *[Peter Newall collection]*

Llandaff City aground in Hung Road, River Avon between 9th and 18th January 1890 and discharging cargo overside into barges. *[West Country Maritime Records - Grahame Farr/World Ship Society Ltd.]*

7. LLANDAFF CITY 1882-1910 Iron
O.N. 85806 1,940g 1,259n 270.2 x 36.0 x 23.5 feet.
C. 2-cyl. (36 and 67 x 36 inches) by Thomas Richardson and Sons, Hartlepool.
7.1882: Launched by Richardson, Duck and Co., Stockton-on-Tees (Yard No.287) for Charles Hill and Sons, Bristol as LLANDAFF CITY.
1909: Laid up at Swansea.
1911: Sold to Companhia Carvoiera de Lisboa, Lisbon, Portugal.
1912: Sold to Dampfer Rhederei Merkur G.m.b.H. (Emil R. Retz, managers), Stettin, Germany and renamed CAESAR.
1914: Laid up at Cartagena.
30.6.1919: Surrendered to the Shipping Controller, London, and subsequently handed over to the French Government, Paris.
1922: Sold to Pittaluga, Genoa, Italy and broken up.

8. WELLS CITY (1) 1882-1887
O.N. 85819 1,960g 1,271n 270.0 x 36.1 x 23.5 feet.
T. 3-cyl. (21.5, 36 and 57 x 36 inches) by Thomas Richardson and Sons, Hartlepool.
7.1885: Launched by the North of England Shipbuilding Co. Ltd., Sunderland (Yard No. 110) for Charles Hill and Sons, Bristol as WELLS CITY.
10.2.1887: Arrived at New York from Bristol and was about to anchor in the Hudson when she was caught by ice flows drifting down the river and swept onto the coastal steamer LONE STAR. Severely damaged, the WELLS CITY sank within 20 minutes.
1887: Salvaged, repaired and sold to the New York and Yucatan Steam Ship

Company, New York, USA and renamed PROGRESO.
1893: Sold to J.M. Waterbury, New York
1894: Sold to the Progreso Steamship Company (James Jerome, manager), New York.
3.12.1902: Destroyed by explosion in fuel tank while lying at a shipyard at Harbor View, San Francisco.
20.12.1902: Hull sold to H.J. Rogers for dismantling.

Exeter City (1). *[Nigel Farrell collection]*

198

Exeter City (1). *[Peter Newall collection]*

9. EXETER CITY (1) 1887-1925

O.N. 91084 2,140g 1,434n 285.0 x 38.0 x 23.9 feet.

T. 3-cyl. (22.5, 37.0 and 61.0 x 42.0 inches) by Blair and Co., Stockton-on-Tees.

12.1887: Completed by the Blyth Shipbuilding Co. Ltd., Blyth (Yard No. 60) for Charles Hill and Sons, Bristol as EXETER CITY.

1919: Owners became the Bristol City Line of Steamships Ltd. (Charles Hill and Sons, managers), Bristol.

6.1925: Broken up by Stablimento Metallurgica Ligure, Genoa, Italy.

10. GLOUCESTER CITY (2) 1889-1902

O.N. 95761 2,193g 1,409n 292.2 x 39.0 x 19.1 feet.

T. 3-cyl. (22.5, 37.0 and 61.0 x 42.0 inches) by Blair and Co., Stockton-on-Tees.

1889: Completed by J.L. Thompson and Sons Ltd., Sunderland (Yard No. 254) for Charles Hill and Sons, Bristol as GLOUCESTER CITY.

1891: Transferred to W.R. Corfield, Bristol.

1904: Sold to Nakajima Ihei, Yokohama, Japan and renamed TAIAN MARU.

1906: Sold to Sampuko Goshi Kaisha, Yokohama.

1908: Sold to Shoshen Kaisha Tomikura Sempakubu, Yokohama.

1912: Sold to Tatsuma Kishen Goshi Kaisha, Nishimoniyo, Japan.

30.7.1913: Wrecked seven miles off Shanghai whilst on a voyage from Chinwangtao to Shanghai with a cargo of coal and cement.

11. WELLS CITY (2) 1890-1928

O.N. 95769 1,814g 1,136n 281.2 x 36.0 x 20.9 feet.

T. 3-cyl. (21.0, 36.0 and 57.0 x 39.0 inches) by Blair and Co., Stockton-on-Tees.

10.1890: Completed by Charles Hill and Sons, Bristol (Yard No. 16) as WELLS CITY.

1919: Owners became the Bristol City Line of Steamships Ltd. (Charles Hill and Sons, managers), Bristol.

1928: Sold to B. Andreakis and G. Neophytos Shipping, Chartering and Forwarding Co. S.A., Piraeus, Greece and renamed KEPHALOS.

1928: Theo Papadimitriou became manager and renamed NEVAS.

1930: Renamed ALMA.

1933: Broken up in Italy during the last quarter of the year.

Wells City (1). *[Roy Fenton collection]*

Chicago City approaching Bristol. *[Ian J. Farquhar collection]*

12. CHICAGO CITY 1892-1929

O.N. 98836 2,324g 1,478n 295.0 x
39.3 x 22.5 feet.
T. 3-cyl. (23.5, 39.0 and 64.0 x 42.0
inches) by Blair and Co., Stockton-on-
Tees.
12.1892: Completed by J. Blumer and
Co., Sunderland (Yard No.125) for
Charles Hill and Sons, Bristol as
CHICAGO CITY.
1919: Owners became the Bristol City
Line of Steamships Ltd. (Charles Hill and
Sons, managers), Bristol.
15.12.1929: Arrived in the Clyde for
breaking up, probably by R. Smith, Port
Glasgow.

13. BOSTON CITY (1) 1893-1904

O.N. 98838 2,345g 1,483n 295.0 x
39.3 x 22.6
T. 3-cyl. (23.5, 39.0 and 64.0 x 42.0
inches) by Blair and Co., Stockton-on-
Tees.
6.1893: Completed by J. Blumer and Co.,
Sunderland (Yard No.126) for Charles
Hill and Sons, Bristol as BOSTON
CITY.
31.1.1904: Sailed from New York for
Bristol off South West Spit, Sandy Hook
collided with the US steamer
COLARDO. Beached at Flynn's Knoll
and abandoned to underwriters.
6.8.1904: Refloated, repaired, sold to
John E. Berwind, New York, USA and
renamed BERWIND.

Boston City (1). *[World Ship Society Ltd.]*

1908: Sold to the New York and Puerto
Rico Steam Ship Company, New York.
3.8.1918: Torpedoed and sunk by the
German submarine UB 88 in position
47.57 north by 04.03 west whilst on a
voyage from St. Nazaire to Barry.

14. KANSAS CITY 1893-1917

O.N. 102481 2,345g 1,482n
295.0 x 39.3 x 22.5 feet.

T 3-cyl. (23.5, 39.0 and 64.0 x 42.0
inches) by Blair and Co., Stockton-on-
Tees.
10.1893: Completed by J. Blumer and
Co., Sunderland (Yard No.127) for
Charles Hill and Sons, Bristol as
KANSAS CITY.
30.8.1917: Left New York for Bristol and
disappeared.
5.9.1917: Last sighted.

Kansas City. [Ian J. Farquhar collection]

15. BATH CITY (2) 1899-1900

O.N. 111301   2,511g 1,606n
310.0 x 40.5 x 22.3 feet.
T 3-cyl. (24.0, 40.0 and 66.0 x 45.0) by
Blair and Co. Ltd., Stockton-on-Tees.
8.1899: Completed by J.L. Thompson
and Sons Ltd., Sunderland (Yard No.372)
for Charles Hill and Sons, Bristol as
BATH CITY.
23.2.1900: Wrecked on Needle Rock at
the north end of Lundy Island and
foundered in deep water whilst on a
voyage from New York to Bristol with
grain and general cargo.

16. BRISTOL CITY (2) 1899-1917

O.N. 111303   2,511g 1,600n
310.0 x 40.5 x 22.6 feet.

Bath City (2), completed in 1899 and lost in 1900. *[World Ship Society Ltd.]*

Bristol City (2) of 1899, torpedoed and sunk in December 1917. *[World Ship Society Ltd.]*

Bristol City (2) in wartime grey.   *[Peter Newall collection]*

T 3-cyl. (24.0, 40.0 and 66.0 x 45.0 inches) by Blair and Co., Stockton-on-Tees.
12.1899: Completed by Charles Hill and Sons Ltd., Bristol (Yard No. 20) for their own account as BRISTOL CITY.
18.12.1917: Torpedoed and sunk by the German submarine U 94 south west of Ireland in position 48.05 north by 09.58 west whilst on a voyage from Bristol to New York with general cargo. 30 were lost.

17. NEW YORK CITY (2) 1907-1915
O.N. 117736   2,970g 1,600n
310.0 x 40.5 x 22.4 feet.
T 3-cyl. (26.0, 42.5 and 69.5 x 45.0 inches) by Blair and Co., Stockton-on-Tees.
8.1907: Completed by Richardson, Duck and Co., Stockton-on-Tees (Yard No. 586) for Charles Hill and Sons, Bristol as NEW YORK CITY.
19.8.1915: Captured by the German submarine U 24 40 miles south south east of Fastnet in position 51.00 north by 08.50 west and sunk by gunfire whilst on a voyage from Bristol and Swansea to New York with general cargo.

18. BOSTON CITY (2) 1917-1918
O.N. 134717   2,736g 1,622n   310.0 x 42.8 x 23.6 feet.
T 3-cyl. (24.0, 39.0 and 66.0 x 45.0 inches) by Richardson, Westgarth and Co., West Hartlepool
2.1917: Completed by Charles Hill and Sons, Bristol, (Yard No. 124) for their own account as BOSTON CITY.

2.1.1918: Torpedoed and sunk by the German submarine U 91 in St. George's Channel, 11 miles west half north of St. Ann's Head, Milford Haven in position 51.40 north by 05.26 west whilst on a voyage from Bristol to New York with general cargo.

19. NEW YORK CITY (3) 1917-1950
O.N. 134720   2,736g 1,622n   310.0 x 42.8 x 23.6 feet.
T 3-cyl. (24.0, 39.0 and 66.0 x 45.0 inches) by Richardson, Westgarth and Co., West Hartlepool.
12.1917: Completed by Charles Hill and Sons, Bristol (Yard No. 125) for their own account as NEW YORK CITY.

1919: Owners became the Bristol City Line of Steamships Ltd. (Charles Hill and Sons, managers), Bristol.
1950: Sold to Kisinbay Birandellar Ltd., Istanbul, Turkey and renamed KAMAL.
1951: Sold to Far Eastern and Panama Transportation Co. Ltd., Panama (Wheelock, Martin and Co., Hong Kong, managers) and renamed WILLA.
1952: Sold to Pacific Union Steam Ship Co. S.A., Panama (Hai Ying Steam Ship Co. Ltd., Hong Kong, managers).
1953: Sold to Poching Navigation Company (People's Republic of China), Shanghai and renamed HOPING 5.
1959: Deleted from 'Lloyd's Register', where still listed as WILLA.

New York City (2). *[Bristol Museum & Art Gallery P3155M / Roy Fenton collection]*

Top: *Boston City* (2) delivered in 1917, torpedoed and sunk in St. George's Channel in 1918. *[Peter Newall collection]*

Middle: *New York City* (3). *[George Scott collection]*

Right: *New York City* (3) armed and in dazzle paint. *[George Scott collection]*

(To be concluded in Record 33)

THE LAST YEARS OF THE LOCH LINE - Part 2
Malcolm Cooper

The Loch Ness was the fastest of the first six ships of the Loch Line, even when cut down to barque rig and with small and indifferent crews. In 1874 she went from the Tuskar to Hobson's Bay, Melbourne in 68 days. *[Monterey Maritime Museum]*

Fleet list

1. LOCH KATRINE 1869-1910 Iron ship
O.N. 60453 1,252g 1,200n 226.0 x 35.8 x 21.5 feet
23.8.1869: Launched by J.G. Lawrie and Co., Whiteinch (Yard No.46) for the Glasgow Shipping Company (Aitken, Lilburn and Co., managers), Glasgow as LOCH KATRINE.
24.9.1869: Registered at Glasgow (108/1869) in the names of James Arthur, Walter Birrell and John Pearson Kidston.
29.4.1910: Dismasted off Cape Howe whilst on a voyage from Melbourne to Sydney.
10.5.1910: Towed into Port Jackson by the tug HEROIC.
17.6.1910: Sold to Dalgety and Co Ltd, Sydney for conversion into a hulk.
14.9.1910: Re-registered at Sydney, New South Wales (26/1910) in the name of Dalgety and Co. Ltd.
9.10.1910: Register annotated to show vessel converted into a lighter.
26.7.1911: Register closed. Vessel subsequently taken to Rabaul, New Britain for use as a copra hulk and eventually sunk as a breakwater.

2. LOCH NESS 1869-1908 Iron ship
O.N. 60461 1,258g 1,203n 225.5 x 35.6 x 21.6 feet
2.9.1869: Launched by Barclay Curle and Co., Stobcross (Yard No.193) for the Glasgow Shipping Company (Aitken, Lilburn and Co., managers), Glasgow as LOCH NESS.
26.10.1869: Registered at Glasgow (126/1869) in the names of James Arthur, Walter Birrell, John Pearson Kidston and Henry James Watson.
22.2.1908: Re-registered at Sydney (38/1908) for sale.
13.8.1908: Sold to George Tarlton Wills, London and immediately re-sold to the Stevedore and Shipping Co. Ltd., Sydney (a subsidiary of Deutsche-Australische Dampfschiffs Gesellschaft, Hamburg) for conversion into a coal hulk.
28.10.1908: Re-registered at Port Adelaide (7/1908) in the name of Stevedore and Shipping Co. Ltd., Sydney.
1914: Seized by the Australian government on the outbreak of war and subsequently towed to Fremantle.
18.8.1926: Sunk in gunfire practice by HMAS MELBOURNE off Rottnest Island, off Fremantle.
9.2.1927: Register closed.

3. LOCH TAY 1869-1909 Iron ship
O.N. 60468 1,250g 1,191n 225.4 x 35.5 x 21.6 feet
23.10.1869: Launched by Barclay Curle and Co., Stobcross (Yard No. 194) for the Glasgow Shipping Company (Aitken, Lilburn and Co., managers), Glasgow as LOCH TAY.
25.11.1869: Registered at Glasgow (135/1869) in the names of James Arthur, Walter Birrell, John Pearson Kidston and Henry James Watson.
2.9.1909: Sold to Huddart Parker and Co. Pty. Ltd., Melbourne for conversion into a coal hulk.
6.10.1909: Re-registered at Sydney (34/1909) in the name of James Lilburn, Glasgow (sale not yet registered).
12.11.1909: Re-registered at Port Adelaide (9/1909) in the name of Huddart Parker and Co. Pty. Ltd., Melbourne.
19.7.1910: Re-registered at Melbourne.
18.10.1912: Re-registered at Port Adelaide (10/1912).
1958: Broken up at Port Adelaide.
24.4.1958: Register closed.

Loch Tay, loaded and ready to sail from the Clyde. Note the houseflag of the Glasgow Shipping Company at the main; it had white 'GSCo.' on a red triangle which tapered to the fly, with remainder of the flag white. *Loch Tay's* hull survived for almost 90 years. *[Robertson-Adamson Marine Collection/John Naylon collection]*

Above left: *Loch Tay* under tow at Adelaide. *[National Maritime Museum P4452]* Above right: *Loch Tay* at Glasgow. *[National Maritime Museum P4454]* Below left and right: A seaman splicing ropes and the sailmaker at work on board the *Loch Tay*. *[National Maritime Museum P7282 and P7281]*

4. LOCH EARN 1869-1873 Iron ship

O.N. 60470 1,248g 1,200n 226.2 x 35.8 x 21.5 feet

20.10.1869: Launched by J.G. Lawrie and Co., Whiteinch (Yard No.47) for the Glasgow Shipping Company (Aitken, Lilburn and Co., managers), Glasgow as LOCH EARN.

15.12.1869: Registered at Glasgow (142/1869) in the names of James Arthur, Walter Birrell, John Pearson Kidston and Henry James Watson.

28.11.1873: Abandoned at sea in a sinking condition in the North Atlantic after sinking the French steamer VILLE DU HAVRE in collision on 21.11.1873; all saved (226 lost with French liner, 87 saved).

5. LOCH LOMOND 1870-1908 Iron ship

O.N. 63741 1,249g 1,200n 226.3 x 35.8 x 21.5 feet

29.1.1870: Launched by J.G. Lawrie and Co., Whiteinch (Yard No.49) for the Glasgow Shipping Company (Aitken, Lilburn and Co., managers), Glasgow as LOCH LOMOND.

22.2.1870: Registered at Glasgow (14/1870) in the names of James Arthur, Walter Birrell, John Pearson Kidston and Henry James Watson.

19.5.1908: Sold to Charles Harvey Cooper, London.

21.5.1908: Re-registered at London (45/1908) in the name of Charles Harvey Cooper.

29.5.1908: Sold to the Union Steam Ship Co. of New Zealand Ltd., Dunedin.

16.7.1908: Sailed from Newcastle New South Wales for Lyttelton, New Zealand with a cargo of coal and disappeared.

23.7.1908: Re-registered at Dunedin (the vessel's loss was not confirmed at this stage).

23.12.1908: Register closed.

6. LOCH LEVEN 1870-1871 Iron ship

O.N. 63759 1,257g 1,200n 225.8 x 35.8 x 21.5 feet

16.3.1870: Launched by J.G. Lawrie and Co., Whiteinch (Yard No.45) for the Glasgow Shipping Co. (Aitken, Lilburn and Co., managers), Glasgow as LOCH LEVEN.

22.4.1870: Registered at Glasgow (40/1870) in the names of James Arthur, Walter Birrell, John Pearson Kidston and Henry James Watson.

24.10.1871: Stranded on Harbinger Reef near Cape Wickham, King Island, Bass Strait whilst on a voyage from Geelong to London with a cargo of 6,523 bales of wool; all landed safely, but master drowned after going back in a surf boat to retrieve ship's papers.

16.5.1872: Register closed.

7. AMERICA/LOCH LAGGAN 1873-1875 Iron ship

O.N. 63874 1,504g 1,435n 243.1 x 37.8 x 22.8 feet

The *Loch Lomond* was known as 'the Scottish man-of-war' in her palmy days owing to her smart appearance under Commander Grey, RNR. *[National Maritime Museum P4443]*

28.2.1872: Launched by Charles Connell and Co., Scotstoun (Yard No.76) for J.H. Watt and Co., Glasgow as AMERICA.

23.3.1872: Registered at Glasgow (29/1872) in the name of John Hugh Watt.

1.1873: Acquired by the General Shipping Company (Aitken, Lilburn and Co., managers), Glasgow.

23.1.1873: Re-registered at Glasgow (2/1873) in the names of James Arthur, John Pearson Kidston, Samuel Macfarlane and James Aitken.

4.1875: Renamed LOCH LAGGAN.

26.4.1875: Re-registered at Glasgow (40/1875) under the same ownership.

1.10.1875: Sailed from Liverpool for Melbourne.

25.11.1875: Spoken to in position 26 south by 25 west and then disappeared.

19.4.1876: Posted missing at Lloyd's.

27.4.1876: Register closed.

8. LOCH MAREE 1873-1881 Iron ship

O.N. 68057 1,657g 1,581n 255.8 x 38.6 x 22.9 feet

23.9.1873: Launched by Barclay, Curle and Co., Stobcross (Yard No.239) for the Glasgow Shipping Co. (Aitken, Lilburn and Co., managers), Glasgow as LOCH MAREE.

3.11.1873: Registered at Glasgow (95/1873) in the names of James Arthur, Walter Birrell, John Pearson Kidston and Henry James Watson.

29.10.1881: Sailed from Geelong for London with a cargo of wheat and disappeared.

5.10.1882: Register closed.

Left: The lofty *Loch Maree* sporting her three skysail yards. Built without regard to expense, she was probably the fastest of all the 'Lochs'.
[Monterey Maritime Museum]

Middle: A superb view of *Loch Ard* in the Thames, 2nd March 1878, before her final and tragic voyage. *[National Maritime Museum; G1553; John Naylon collection]*

Bottom: There were only two survivors from the wreck of *Loch Ard* in 1878. Thomas Pearce (left) rescued Evaline Carmichael (right), and wears the gold medal he received from the Royal Humane Society. *[Flagstaff Hill Maritime Village; Author's collection]*

9. LOCH ARD 1873-1878 Iron ship
O.N. 68061 1,693g 1,624n 262.7 x 38.3 x 23.0 feet
8.11.1873: Launched by Charles Connell and Co., Scotstoun (Yard No.87) for the General Shipping Company (Aitken, Lilburn and Co., managers), Glasgow as LOCH ARD.
28.11.1873: Registered at Glasgow (101/1873) in the names of James Arthur, John Pearson Kidston, Samuel Macfarlane and James Aitken.
1.6.1878: Wrecked near Curdies Inlet, 27 miles west of Cape Otway, whilst on a voyage from London to Melbourne with general cargo; 50 lost, 2 survivors.
25.11.1878: Register closed.

10. LOCH RANNOCH 1875-1907
Iron ship
O.N. 60354 1,243g 1,185n 217.8 x
35.5 x 21.0 feet
4.6.1868: Launched by J. and G.
Thomson and Co., Govan (Yard No.101)
for Kidston and Co., Glasgow as CLAN
RANALD.
26.6.1868: Registered at Glasgow (69/
1868) in the names of John Pearson
Kidston, William Ferrier-Kerr and John
Black.
2.1875: Acquired by the Glasgow
Shipping Company (Aitken, Lilburn and
Co., managers), Glasgow and renamed
LOCH RANNOCH.
19.2.1875: Re-registered at Glasgow (16/
1875) in the names of James Arthur,
Walter Birrell, John Pearson Kidston and
Henry James Watson.
1907: Sold to Acties. Loch Rannoch (M
Nielsen, manager), Laurvig, Norway.
17.8.1907: Register closed.
19.10.1909: Arrived at Hamburg and
subsequently sold for breaking up at
Harburg.

11. LOCH VENNACHAR 1875-1905
Iron ship
O.N. 71748 1,557g 1,485n 250.1 x
38.3 x 22.4 feet
4.8.1875: Launched by J. and G.
Thomson and Co., Clydebank (Yard
No.139) for the Glasgow Shipping
Company (Aitken, Lilburn and Co.,
managers), Glasgow as LOCH
VENNACHAR.
25.8.1875: Registered at Glasgow (89/
1875) in the names of James Arthur,
Walter Birrell, John Pearson Kidston and
Henry James Watson.
12.11.1901: Run down and sunk by the
British steamer CATO (1,090/1867)
while at anchor off Thameshaven. Later
raised and towed to Tilbury for repairs.
6.9.1905: Spoken in position 35.21 south
by 133 east, 160 miles west of Neptune
Island whilst on a voyage from Glasgow

Above: *Loch Vennachar. [Glasgow University Archives DC101/0730]* Below:
Loch Vennachar being raised off Thameshaven in 1901 following her collision with
the *Cato. [National Maritimre Museum P4466]*

to Adelaide and Melbourne with general
cargo (sailed on 14.6.1905) and then
disappeared; 27 lost, wreckage
subsequently discovered on Kangaroo

Island and wreck found there by divers in
1976.
8.11.1905: Posted missing at Lloyd's.
13.11.1905: Register closed

12. LOCH GARRY 1875-1911 Iron ship
O.N. 73788 1,565g 1,493n 250.5 x 38.4 x 22.6 feet
1.10.1875: Launched by J. and G. Thomson and Co., Clydebank (Yard No.140) for the Glasgow Shipping Company (Aitken, Lilburn and Co., managers), Glasgow as LOCH GARRY.
23.10.1875: Registered at Glasgow (121/ 1875) in the names of James Arthur, Walter Birrell, John Pearson Kidston and Henry James Watson.
3.1911: Sold for £1,800 to be broken up in Italy.
9.6.1911: Register closed.
24.8.1911: Arrived at Genoa for breaking up.

13. LOCH FYNE 1876-1883 Iron ship
O.N. 73870 1,270g 1,213n 228.5 x 35.8 x 21.3 feet
5.10.1876: Launched by J. and G. Thomson and Co., Clydebank (Yard No.149) for the General Shipping Company (Aitken, Lilburn and Co., managers), Glasgow as LOCH FYNE.
1.11.1876: Registered at Glasgow (92/ 1876) in the names of James Arthur, John Pearson Kidston, Samuel Macfarlane and James Aitken.
14.5.1883: Sailed from Lyttelton, New Zealand for the Channel with a cargo of 15,000 bags of wheat and disappeared
5.12.1883: Posted missing at Lloyd's.
31.12.1883: Register closed.

Top: *Loch Garry* under tow. She was one of the few Loch Line vessels which was broken up, rather than wrecked. *[Glasgow University Archives DC101/0726 / Rick Hogben collection]*
Bottom: *Loch Fyne,* sister ship to the *Loch Long.* *[Monterey Maritime Museum]*

209

14. LOCH LONG 1876-1903 Iron ship

O.N. 76726 1,261g 1,203n 228.5 x 35.8 x 21.3 feet

20.11.1876: Launched by J. and G. Thomson and Co., Clydebank (Yard No.148) for the General Shipping Company (Aitken, Lilburn and Co., managers), Glasgow as LOCH LONG.

9.12.1876: Registered at Glasgow (105/1876) in the names of James Arthur, John Pearson Kidston, Samuel Macfarlane and James Aitken.

29.4.1903: Sailed from New Caledonia for Glasgow with a cargo of nickel ore and disappeared; 24 lost, wreckage washed up on the Chatham Islands.

11.11.1903: Posted missing at Lloyd's.

20.11.1903: Register closed.

15. LOCH RYAN 1877-1909 Iron ship

O.N. 76738 1,264g 1,207n 228.5 x 35.8 x 21.3 feet

31.1.1877: Launched by J. and G. Thomson and Co., Clydebank (Yard No.150) for the General Shipping Company (Aitken, Lilburn and Co., managers), Glasgow as LOCH RYAN.

26.2.1877: Registered at Glasgow (21/1877) in the names of James Arthur, John Pearson Kidston, Samuel Macfarlane and James Aitken.

1.12.1909: Sold to the Government of the State of Victoria, Melbourne for use as a training ship.

19.1.1910: Re-registered at Melbourne (1/1910) in the name of the Government of the State of Victoria.

20.4.1910: Renamed JOHN MURRAY.

11.12.1917: Sold to the Commonwealth of Australia, re-rigged and returned to service.

29.5.1918: Wrecked on Maldon Islands, South Pacific whilst on a voyage from San Francisco to Melbourne with a general cargo.

8.7.1918: Register closed.

Above: *Loch Long* moored off Gravesend in her original full rig. *[National Maritime Museum P4445]*

Above: *Loch Long* rigged down as a barque. *[National Maritime Museum P4444]*
Below: 1,200-tonners were a favourite size with Aitken, Lilburn. The *Loch Ryan* was not as sharp-ended as her predecessors and was more of a carrier. *[Glasgow University Archives DC101/0728]*

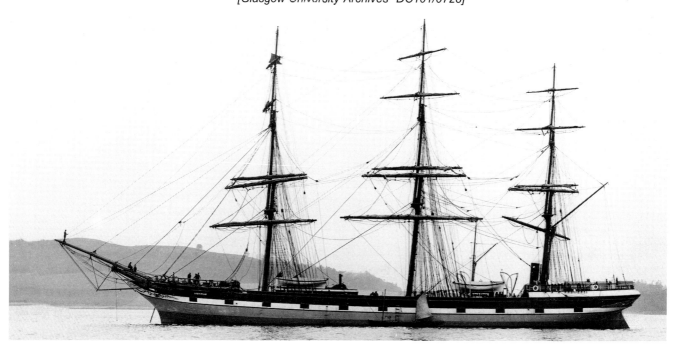

16. LOCH SLOY 1877-1899 Iron ship

O.N. 78562 1,280g 1,225n 225.5 x
35.6 x 21.2 feet
6.11.1877: Launched by D. and W.
Henderson and Co., Meadowside, Partick
(Yard No.178) for the Glasgow Shipping
Company (Aitken, Lilburn and Co.,
managers), Glasgow as LOCH SLOY.
3.12.1877: Registered at Glasgow (131/
1877) in the names of James Arthur,
Walter Birrell, Henry James Watson and
George Jardine Kidston.
24.4.1899: Wrecked at Maupertius Bay,
Kangaroo Island whilst on a voyage from
Glasgow to Adelaide and Melbourne with
a general cargo; 4 survivors of whom 1
died before rescue.
29.5.1899: Register closed.

17. LOCH ETIVE 1878-1911 Iron ship

O.N. 78565 1,288g 1,235n 226.9 x
35.9 x 21.6 feet
22.11.1877: Launched by A. and J. Inglis,
Pointhouse (Yard No.134) for the General
Shipping Company (Aitken, Lilburn and
Co., managers), Glasgow as LOCH
ETIVE.
3.1.1878: Registered at Glasgow (1/1878)
in the names of James Arthur, John
Pearson Kidston, Samuel Macfarlane and
James Aitken.
1911: Sold for £1,350 to be broken up in
Italy.
19.7.1911: Register closed.
7.10.1911: Arrived at Genoa for breaking
up.

18. LOCH SHIEL 1878-1894 Iron ship

O.N. 78568 1,277g 1,218n 225.3 x
35.7 x 21.2 feet
6.12.1877: Launched by D. and W.
Henderson and Co., Meadowside, Partick
(Yard No.179) for the Glasgow Shipping
Company (Aitken, Lilburn and Co.,
managers), Glasgow as LOCH SHIEL.
19.1.1878: Registered at Glasgow (3/
1878) in the names of James Arthur,
Walter Birrell, Henry James Watson and
George Jardine Kidston.
30.1.1894: Stranded on Thorn Island,
Milford Haven whilst on a voyage from
Glasgow to Adelaide and Melbourne with
a general cargo.
24.2.1894: Register closed.

19. LOCH SUNART 1878-1879 Iron ship

O.N. 78573 1,284g 1,231n 225.0 x
35.8 x 21.6 feet
19.1.1878: Launched by A. and J. Inglis,
Pointhouse (Yard No.135) for the General
Shipping Company (Aitken, Lilburn and
Co., managers), Glasgow as LOCH
SUNART.
25.2.1878: Registered at Glasgow (14/
1878) in the names of James Arthur, John
Pearson Kidston, Samuel Macfarlane and
James Aitken.

18.1.1879: Stranded on Skullmartin Reef,
Ballywater Bay, County Down whilst on
a voyage from Glasgow to Melbourne
with a general cargo.
1.3.1879: Register closed.

20. LOCH MOIDART 1881-1890 Iron four-masted barque

O.N. 85856 2,081g 2,000n 287.4 x
42.6 x 24.0 feet
9.9.1881: Launched by Barclay, Curle
and Co., Whiteinch (Yard No.302) for the
General Shipping Company (Aitken,
Lilburn and Co., managers), Glasgow as
LOCH MOIDART.
5.10.1881: Registered at Glasgow (89/
1881) in the names of Samuel Macfarlane
and James Aitken.
27.1.1890: Wrecked at Callantzoog,
Nieuwe Diep whilst on a voyage from
Pisagua to Hamburg with a cargo of
nitrate; two saved.
29.5.1890: Register closed.

Top: *Loch Shiel* was sister to the *Loch Sloy*. *[Monterey Maritime Museum]*
Bottom: The short-lived *Loch Moidart* was sister to the *Loch Torridon*. These
were the first two four-masted barques in the fleet. *[John Naylon collection]*

Above left: *Loch Torridon* at anchor. Commanded by Captain R. Pattman for over 26 years, the *Loch Torridon* was one of the best-known and fastest four-masted barques in the British merchant marine. *[National Maritime Museum P411]* Above right: *Loch Torridon*. *[J. & M. Clarkson collection]* Bottom: *Loch Broom* for the greater part of her career was commanded by Bully Martin, 'a driver of the old type' according to Lubbock. *[National Maritime Museum P401]*

21. LOCH TORRIDON 1881-1912
Iron four-masted barque
O.N. 85876   2,081g 2,000n   287.4 x 42.6 x 24.0 feet
9.11.1881: Launched by Barclay, Curle and Co., Whiteinch (Yard No.303) for the General Shipping Company (Aitken, Lilburn and Co., managers), Glasgow as LOCH TORRIDON.
22.12.1881: Registered at Glasgow (128/1881) in the names of Samuel Macfarlane and James Aitken.
1912: Sold to A. E. Blom, Nystad, Denmark.
8.7.1912: Register closed.

24.1.1915: Abandoned dismasted and in a sinking condition in position 51.35 north by 12.28 west whilst on a voyage from Fredrikstad to Geelong with a cargo of timber.

22. LOCH BROOM 1885-1912 Iron four-masted barque
O.N. 90017   2,128g 2,075n   287.7 x 42.5 x 24.1 feet
17.2.1885: Launched by Barclay, Curle and Co., Whiteinch (Yard No.333) for the General Shipping Company (Aitken, Lilburn and Co., managers), Glasgow as LOCH BROOM.

7.4.1885: Registered at Glasgow (31/1885) in the names of James Aitken and James Lilburn.
8.1912: Sold to Skibsakties. Songdal (S.O. Stray and Co., managers), Christiansand, Norway and renamed SONGDAL.
19.8.1912: Register closed.
1916: Transferred to A/S Christiansand (S.O. Stray and Co., managers), Christiansand.
2.2.1917: Sunk by the German submarine U 81 south west of Ireland in position 50.10 north by 10.10 west whilst on a voyage from Buenos Aires to London with a cargo of maize.

Above: *Loch Carron* at Lyttelton in 1890. Although very fast, she was rather tender and Captain Stainton Clarke always sent her royal yards down in port. *[National Maritime Museum P402]*

Right: Damage to the bows and headgear of the *Loch Carron* after her collision with the *Inverkip* on 13th August 1904. *[National Maritime Museum P4420]*

23. LOCH CARRON 1885-1912 Iron four-masted barque

O.N. 90033 2,128g 2,075n 287.7 x 42.5 x 24.1 feet

15.4.1885: Launched by Barclay, Curle and Co., Whiteinch (Yard No.334) for the General Shipping Company (Aitken, Lilburn and Co., managers), Glasgow as LOCH CARRON.

12.5.1885: Registered at Glasgow (48/1885) in the names of James Aitken and James Lilburn.

6.1912: Sold to A/S Christiansand (S.O. Stray and Co., managers), Christiansand, Norway and renamed SEILEREN.

17.6.1912: Register closed.

11.10.1915: Sunk in collision with the British steamer VITTORIA (2,817/1907) three miles off Torr Head, County Antrim whilst on a voyage from Greenock to Delaware Breakwater in ballast.

**24. LOCH NEVIS 1894-1900 Steel
four-masted barque**
O.N. 104525 2,431g 2,328n 301.7 x
43.2 x 24.6 feet
5.6.1894: Launched by John Reid and
Co. Ltd., Whiteinch (Yard No.277) for
the General Shipping Company (Aitken,
Lilburn and Co., managers), Glasgow as
LOCH NEVIS.
20.6.1894: Registered at Glasgow (64/
1894) in the name of James Lilburn.
9.1900: Sold to Rhederei Acties
Gesellschaft von 1896, Hamburg,
Germany and renamed OCTAVIA.
15.9.1900: Register closed.
6.8.1905: Beached at Bahia Blanca,
Patagonia after an explosion in her cargo
of coal; salved and converted into a hulk
at Puerto Madryn.
1918: Rebuilt as a steamer using
machinery from the steamer KAISER
(2,724/1891) for Gaddo Cappagli,
Buenos Aires and renamed PRIMERO.
17.8.1922: Wrecked at Deseado near
Penguin Island whilst on a voyage from
Valparaiso to Buenos Aires with a
general cargo.

Above: *Loch Nevis.* In contrast to Aitken, Lilburn's earlier skysail yarders, the last
of their ships was a big stump-topgallant carrier lifting 4,000 tons deadweight. *[J.
& M. Clarkson collection]*
Below: *Loch Nevis* under tow in the Clyde. *[Glasgow University Archives DC101/
0727]*

FURNESS-HOULDER FOLLOW UP

Much correspondence has been generated by the late Dennis Johnzon's masterly account of the Furness-Houlder meat ships, which appeared in *Records* 29 to 31.

Abadesa omission
There is just one omission in the coverage of the Furness-Houlder fleet in *Record* 29; *Abadesa* of 1916 was laid down as *Dominion Miller* for Norfolk and North American Steamship Company but was transferred to Furness-Houlder Argentine Lines and renamed *Abadesa* during construction, consequent on Furness having purchased her owners. This is mentioned in David Burrell's 'Furness Withy 1891-1991' and also in the Starke-Schell Registers.
GEORGE ROBINSON, Southwood Cottage, 79 Southwood Road, Cottingham HU16 5AJ

Manchester matters
Assuming the stated beam measurement of the *El Argentino* to be correct ('The Furness Withy - Houlder Brothers Link - Part 2' in *Record* 30), then she would have been too wide to have visited Manchester. At 64.5 feet she would have been technically within the 65 feet width of the upper locks on the Ship Canal but in practice there would have been insufficient clearance for her to be safely and efficiently worked through.

As far as I know, the widest ships ever to visit Manchester were the Strick Line sisters *Registan* and *Serbistan* of 1966 at 63 feet 10 inches, closely followed by the Manchester Liners' *Challenge* class container vessels at 63 feet 9 inches. Most of the conventional cargo liners built down to a size to fit the Ship Canal were less than 63 feet 6 inches.

It seems odd, then, that Manchester Liners chose the *El Argentino* for their continued investment in the South American meat trade. She seems wide in relation to her length and when compared with the dimensions of her older near-sisters.

On a completely different subject, but still related to the Port of Manchester, in *Record* 8 I noticed in a review of 'Old Order, New Thing' a statement which raised my hackles, namely that 'The (Manchester Ship) canal was hardly ever used for its avowed purpose of importing cotton'. Raw cotton was, of course, a major cargo at Manchester Docks, coming in not only from US Gulf and Atlantic ports (in ships of Harrison Line and others) but also from other countries including Venezuela, India and Egypt.
KEN LOWE, 4 Ansells, Seaview, Isle of Wight PO34 5JL
The statement that the Ship Canal was never, to any large extent, used for importing cotton into Manchester is that of the author of 'Old Order, New Thing', Campbell McMurray. His conclusion is supported by the work of David Farnie in 'The Manchester Ship Canal and the Rise of the Port of Manchester', probably the best study of the Ship Canal's trade. Cotton certainly was carried to Manchester by the canal, peaking at about 35% of the total volume of UK imports of this commodity in 1938-39. But the canal did not, as its promoters hoped, seriously challenge Liverpool's dominance in the cotton trade. Farnie believes this was largely because Liverpool retained the market where cotton was bought and sold, because it had cotton merchants and brokers, a cotton exchange, banks to finance cotton imports and appropriate warehouses, all of which Manchester lacked. Ed.

Chilled or frozen
On page 131 of *Record* 31 Denis Johnzon comments on the war-built *Condesa*, saying '…seem to indicate that at first she was equipped to carry frozen meat only...'. In both world wars the British Government took control of meat supplies from Argentina, buying everything they could and, at times, diverting supplies to our Allies. All the meat was frozen down hard as that enabled the maximum cargo to be stowed. Chilled meat was hung from rails and was very wasteful on space. Come peace, the trade gradually returned to private hands and the ships were refitted for chilled cargo.

In 'Lloyd's List' for 13th March 1953 there is a report that *Paraguay Star* was due that day with 160 tons of chilled meat, the first from Argentina since 1939. 'Lloyd's List' for 11th June 1955 records the arrival of the first private beef shipments since before the war. The issue for 6th January 1955 records *Highland Princess's* arrival with 1,540 tons of chilled beef, a post-war record shipment.
DAVID BURRELL, 6 Glaisnock View, Cumnock, Ayrshire KA18 3GA

Duquesa's machinery
Of special interest to me is the Furness-Houlder refrigerated cargo ship *Duquesa*, a superb example of the class of ship we excelled in building.

Turbine-powered, a feature of her boiler installation was the provision of automatic combustion control equipment, one of the first such installations in a British ship. In addition her two casing turbines, designed in collaboration with the Pametrada organisation, comprised an all-impulse high-pressure cylinder, which did not incorporate an astern turbine, whilst the low-pressure cylinder of impulse-reaction type had a two-row impulse astern turbine incorporated within a cast steel housing but separate from the low-pressure ahead casing.
GEORGE SHOTTER, 16 Aboyne Avenue, Orton Waterville, Peterborough PE2 5ET

Elusive emigrant numbers
Houlders were never a prime passenger-carrying line, but in their earlier years did take passengers (mostly emigrants) in their ships to Australia. Then, of course, the emphasis shifted to South America, with a similar pattern of shipping out emigrants in rudimentary quarters variously described as third class, dormitory, 'tween-decks or steerage. Services thrived in the years before the outbreak of the First World War, with lines such as Shaw Savill, Tysers and Roydens to Australia and Houlders and Royal Mail to South America being prominent. The Royal Mail ships would call at Spanish ports such as Vigo and Bilbao to pick up emigrants on the way south. Quarters could be cleared for the return voyage, when passengers were few, by removing temporary partitions to enable the deck space to be used for cargo. The passenger facilities would only be brought into use when there was a demand, which was often intermittent. Some ships may even have been fitted out with temporary passenger quarters which were not used at all before war broke out.

Information on these one-way services is often difficult to pin down, as many writers do not include such emigrant carriers in any compendium of passenger ships. To me, any paying traveller, on board for whatever reason, is a 'passenger' and these ships are of equal interest to the regular liners. In the case of Houlders, the main group comprised the five completed in 1912-13, mentioned on page 3 of *Record* 29. Although two (*El Paraguayo* and *La Correntina*) were built for Houlder Line itself and three (*El Paraguayo*, *La Rosarina* and *La Negra*) for the offshoot British and Argentine Steam Navigation, they were essentially almost identical sisterships. All carried enough lifeboats (anything from 6 to 10 in different photographs) to give the appearance of passenger carriers. The variance in numbers of boats may relate to whether emigrants or steerage were being carried at the time of the shot. Of the other three, only *La Negra* was listed as carrying other than 12 first-class passengers. However, N.R.P. Bonsor in his 'South Atlantic Seaway' shows all five as taking 400 third as well as 12 first. One supposes the former accommodation was brought into use only on demand, but

Bonsor gives no detail as to actual use or numbers carried, as he did so well in 'North Atlantic Seaway'.
ROBERT H. LANGLOIS, Feu Follet, Maisons au Compte Road, Vale, Guernsey GY3 5HF

Love for 'the little rose'
The articles on the Furness Withy-Houlder Brothers link had a very special significance for me as in the 1930s my father, Charles Johnson, spent the early part of his seagoing career as an engineer with this fleet.

After an apprenticeship with the Liverpool-based ship repairers A. and R. Brown Ltd., in 1930 he signed on as Seventh Engineer on *El Paraquayo* for a voyage from Liverpool to the River Plate. The size and breakdown of the crew of 98 suggests that she was to carry both passengers and live animals.

His next voyage was as Fifth Engineer on the *Sutherland Grange*, sailing on 6th December 1930 to Patagonia from Tollesbury in Essex. She was coming out of lay up on the River Blackwater, Houlder's *Oaklands Grange* arriving the same day to take her place in lay up. The crew of 64 had to provide their own bedding. The most interesting of my father's photographs from this voyage shows *Sutherland Grange* navigating an extremely tight passage. When he gave me this photograph he told me it was taken at 'Kirkie Narrows', but I suspect this is properly named Albuquerque Narrows, and situated somewhere in the Magellan Strait. Can anyone give a precise location?

After an eight month spell ashore, Charles signed up as Seventh Engineer on *La Rosarina*. Thus began my father's love affair with 'the little rose' which lasted for five years, each year seeing her make four round trips between Liverpool and the River Plate. Between February 1932 and March 1937, La *Rosarina* always ran from Liverpool to Buenos Aires and La Plata, most voyages including calls at Montevideo both outward and homeward, and homeward Rio Grande do Sul, Santos and Santa Cruz de Teneriffe. During this time Charles rose from Seventh to Fourth Engineer. When *La Rosarina* was sold to Japanese

shipbreakers in 1937, my father was so angry with the company that he resigned from Furness-Houlder and went sailing with T. and J. Harrison Ltd. When I look at the Crew Agreements, I begin to see why the ship's demise had such a profound effect. The ship's crew saw very little change in personnel over his five years of service, so the end of the ship meant the end of a family. 'Son', he was wont to tell me, 'that ship was so good there was nothing else like her in the world. The Japanese bought her so they could copy her because she was so well built and they had nothing like her themselves'. It was many years later that I realised he had been talking about a 25-year-old ship. And he never once mentioned that she had gone for scrap.
RON JOHNSON, 129 Raven Meols Lane, Formby, Merseyside L37 4DE

***Condesa* corrections**
Whilst Dennis was correct in stating that *Condesa* of 1944 (*Record* 31, page 133) was built with 473,170 cubic feet of refrigerated space in 22 compartments, this was never altered and I do not know where Dennis's later figure of 550,300 cubic feet came from. Because of wartime restrictions, the *Condesa* was, as the company records relate, built with a skeleton system of insulation. This meant no insulation in numbers 1 and 6 holds, or in number 7 'tween deck. There were no separate meat lockers in the insulated 'tween decks and no meat rails were fitted for the carriage of chilled beef. In other words, the ship could carry only frozen beef and lamb, in numbers 2, 3, 4 and 5 holds and 'tween decks.

Because of the uncertainties which prevailed in the Argentine meat business, *Condesa* was never altered. When on long-term charter to Shaw, Savill, the uninsulated holds and 'tween decks were used mainly for the carriage of bales of wool. Incidentally, the *Rippingham Grange* (page 135) was built as a fully-refrigerated vessel.
JOHN B. HILL, The Hollies, Wall, Hexham, Northumberland NE46 4EQ

Sutherland Grange navigating Albuquerque Narrows in the Magellan Straits in February or March 1931. The master had given some members of the crew permission to go ashore to take this photograph. *[Ron Johnson]*

Leven Grange model

The photograph of the model ship named 'Leven Grange' housed at the Hull Trinity House School gives some idea of what the ex-Argentine Cargo Line steamers *La Blanca* and *El Argentino* looked like in Houlder colours (*Record* 29, page 5). Compared with these ships, on the model the two forward lifeboats have transom sterns, there are gunport doors at upper 'tween deck level at numbers 2 and 4 holds and a gunport door into the bridge space just forward of the gangway.

Regarding the lower photograph on page 5 of *Record* 29, on the older type refrigerated ships the round, solid pillars were bound with rope as can clearly be seen and the box-shaped pillars had a timber fencing built around them to keep the frozen cargo from coming into contact with the metal. The narrow tube on the right was where a thermometer would be lowered to obtain the temperature during the carriage of refrigerated cargo. These tubes were removed when general cargo was carried in the space.
CAPTAIN EDWARD BUCKLE, 67 Beech Road, Elloughton, East Yorkshire HU15 1JY

The model ship named 'Leven Grange' housed at the Hull Trinity House School. Thanks to headmaster A. Twait and Captain C. Anderson for arranging the visit and the photograph. *[Captain Edward Buckle]*

PUTTING THE RECORD STRAIGHT

Letters, additions, amendments and photographs relating to articles in any issues of *Record* are welcomed. Letters may be lightly edited. Communications by e-mail are welcome, but senders are asked to include their postal address.

Conflict over Cape Town

Record 30 was for me the best to date and I would mention a few points.

As recently as ten years ago there was a Lilburn with some of the company's records living in Aboyne.

Page 72: in the top picture *Marquesa* is in the Gourock Anchorage with Kilcreggan and Strone Hill in the background.

Page 72: mid picture can hardly be Cape Town as the tug alongside is almost certainly *Atlantic Cock*, a London river tug.

Page 77: the top picture of *Loch Carron* I am sure is not Cape Town for the following reasons:

1. Neither the left or right background relate to anywhere on the South African coast and certainly not Cape Town. The left background is clearly industrial and that on the right is a long riverfront cargo shed with four towers and a chimney behind. The towers I would suggest are part of a large hydraulic system such as existed on the older and southern section of the Mersey Docks. None of this existed at Cape Town.

2. If this picture was indeed Cape Town, the ship must be moving westward, in which case the background would have to show either The Lions Rump or Head or the even greater massif of Table Mountain.

3. In looking at the ship itself, the extreme cleanliness of the hull and especially boot-topping is virtually proof that she has recently emerged from dry dock and could be crossing the Mersey to complete loading in Birkenhead, or proceeding to Eastham for Ellesmere Port.

4. I know little about sailing ships, but all yards have their sails bent except the fore main, which may even be in process of being shipped (halfway up the after side of the lower foremast). If this is correct the ship may even be ready for sea and only towing into a suitable part of the river to adjust compasses.

5. Although it is suggested a two-funnelled tug was at Cape Town until 1910, all photos that I have seen of the South African harbour craft, prior to them having green bands on the funnels, showed a plain buff funnel with no markings. The tug in the photo clearly has a black top to both funnels. There is however a similarity to the salvage tug *Bullgar* (1) as per *Record* 12, pages 255/6.

6. Wherever the picture was taken, and I strongly lean to the Mersey, it must have been pre-1912 when the *Loch Carron* was sold to Norway. Perhaps a Mersey expert could identify the background.
ARCHIE MUNRO, Chindwin, 6 The Esplanade, Greenock PA16 7XJ

One small correction concerning the caption to the middle photograph of *Marquesa* on page 72. I very much doubt that this was taken off Cape Town. The tug alongside bears no resemblance to any of the South African Railways and Harbour tugs of that period. Also, as the vessel is not flying a courtesy flag at the foremast, it seems more than likely that the photograph was taken off a UK port, particularly as she is flying the pilotage flag (horizontal white and red) from the triatic stay, rather than the International Code Flag H (vertical white and red) which would more probably be flown abroad to indicate that she was carrying a pilot.

Nothing wrong, however, with the photo on page 77 of *Loch Carron* sailing from Cape Town. The tug in the background making all the smoke is most probably the *F.E. Fuller*, built by David J. Dunlop of Glasgow in 1898 for the Table Bay Harbour Board. She was the only two-funnelled tug operating in Cape Town until 1910. She was then sold to the Portuguese Government and was stationed in Lourenco Marques as the *Magul*.
DAVID WITTRIDGE, 25 Fairlawn Close, Rownhams, Southampton SO16 8DT
The middle photograph of Marquesa *on page 72 certainly shows her in the London river; apologies for this slip, and thanks also to Brian W. Hollman and to Tony Shaw for pointing out that it was not taken at Cape Town. However, in the case of the* Loch Carron *shot on page 77, there is clearly a conflict of views. The photographer responsible, Solomon, certainly worked at Cape Town, but as a sailing ship enthusiast may have acquired the negative from another photographer. Contributor Peter Newall knows the port well, and believes it is not Cape Town. Can any reader resolve this conflict, and identify the location? Ed.*

Grain and grain traders

I greatly enjoyed the article on British-built Greek tramps in *Record* 8 as it brought back memories of some of the ships which brought grain to Leith. They included the *Doris* (and thank you for explaining why her funnel colours were different from the majority of the Embiricos fleet, something which had puzzled me for years) and the very smart *Pindar*. Until the new entrance lock was built in the mid-1960s, grain for Leith was brought in ships which had size restrictions imposed on them by the discharge berths, something which was common to a number of other grain-importing ports in the UK. Liberty ships represented the maximum size which could be handled at the silos in the Edinburgh Dock (which was more frequently used only by coasters) and the Imperial Dock. The more recent mill berth opened by Ranks in the Western Harbour (then outside the enclosed system) had broadly similar restrictions, mainly because the berth was tidal and larger ships arriving fully-laden risked taking the bottom at low water.

Canadian wheat came from the St Lawrence or the Great Lakes or (in its short season) from Churchill in a variety of ships, mostly British tramps owned by the likes of Stag Line or Dalgliesh. These shipments were supplemented by the regular fortnightly arrivals of Cairn Line ships whose general cargo often sat above parcels of up to 2,000 tons of grain in the lower tween-decks. Shipments from Mexico, the Plate, Australia or South Africa came in a wider selection of tonnage; perhaps the most frequently-seen British owner was Headlam of Whitby.

As an aside, one occasional visitor was the particularly attractive Italian *Silvio*, registered in Palermo, which neatly fitted the maximum size for the Imperial Dock silo. Cargill used her on more than one occasion and took her again on a voyage charter a year or so later: unfortunately nobody had spotted that she had been lengthened since her last visit and there was great consternation when she arrived off the port and people realised that she was now too long for the berth! After hurried negotiations it was reluctantly decided to allow her to enter the docks although her forward section overhung the berth by many feet and her bow thus interfered with the channel linking the Imperial Dock to the Albert Dock. My memory is that a tug had to be on standby every time a ship (even a small coaster) went through the cut between the docks during the three or four days it took to discharge the grain!

When the new entrance lock had been opened, and much larger ships could use both the Imperial silo and the Rank's mill berth, there was a brief period when ships brought up to 25,000 tons to Leith, usually involving both berths for part-discharges. But the UK's entry into the EEC, and the growing trend to bring much larger ships to continental ports and serve British ports by transhipment (initially sometimes using redundant colliers), brought a major change to the pattern and it became rare to see a grain ship of any size coming to Leith. Indeed, virtually the last time grain was handled at Leith in ships above the 6,000 deadweight size was in the 1980s and early 1990s when 20,000-ton shipments were loaded for export, often to north Africa or the eastern Mediterranean.

I much enjoyed in *Record* 9 the history of Trader Navigation, whose ships were occasional visitors to Leith in the 1950s and early 1960s. On page 13 mention is made of the *Scottish Trader* having been sold and having taken a Fedcom name with Burnett Steamship as managers. The wording of the caption suggests the writer was not aware that Burnett had by then become a wholly-owned subsidiary of the Canadian giant - there had been some sort of association (perhaps a minority shareholding) before that.

On page 15 I was surprised that no mention was made of a dramatic event in the life of the *Middlesex Trader* in 1969 during the brief period when she was named *Homer*. I am almost certain that her new owners were Lyras Brothers - certainly their naming scheme included classical Greek authors. On what I think was her first voyage for her new owners, she was involved in a massive collision in the Thames and berthed at the Tilbury Grain Terminal (then

itself pretty new) with most of her bow smashed almost unrecognisably out of shape. I knew someone then working at the terminal and managed to get permission to go to see her while she was discharging. The incident made the national press at the time and I have certainly not seen at first hand a ship with such extensive damage. I think the owners decided that repairs would be uneconomic and sold her in a damaged state - hence her renaming so soon after her original sale by Trader Navigation.

In his article on Nile Steamship Company in *Record 20*, David Burrell mentions that their *Jutland* was sold in 1953 to Tsavliris (among the smaller, but then quite active, of the London-based Greek tramp owners), then became the *Berna* of a one-ship company managed by S. Catsell and Co., and was repossessed by Tsavliris less than three years later.

I remember her well during her spell as *Berna* as she spent much of that time laid-up in the Imperial Dock in Leith. I was around 11 years old and just beginning to become seriously interested in shipping: my interest, then as now, was more in the companies that owned them and their economic history rather than in the statistics of the ships themselves. The *Berna* was berthed with her stern to the eastern quay of the dock, her bow being secured to a heavy buoy laid specially for the purpose; her presence made it quite awkward to get ships into the busy grain berth which was parallel to her. Access was by an off-puttingly long ladder up to her transom stern.

I never came across any other ships with which S. Catsell and Co was associated and wonder if anybody knows anything of the firm. At the time, I was frustrated to be able to discover nothing about the operators of a ship which I saw so frequently on my regular cycle trips round Leith in those formative years: and I have discovered nothing in the half-century since!
COLIN MENZIES, 17 Bickenhall Mansions, London W1U 6BP

I've got a little list
Many thanks for *Record* 31 and, as usual, good to the last drop. I refer to Tony Smythe's opportune remarks on the final page in respect of listing timber ships. *Record* would never be guilty of the offence but I've seen other maritime caption writers, who should know better, asserting that the timber cargo has shifted when explaining ships photographed at various alarming angles of heel. As Tony says, the culprit is ambitious deck loading that takes little account of the effect on metacentric height of a combination of the water absorption property of softwood and the effect of emptying fuel and water tanks in the bottom of the ship. When my father used to take us down to Garston Dock we very often saw ships arriving in this condition and my brother and I were told by him that this was because the vessel had been allowed to become top-heavy through either ignorance or greed. The ship wasn't overloaded and the cargo certainly hadn't shifted.

I would guess that those unfortunate ships just did not have adequate stability information to hand or the master and his mates were not up to the formidable amount of arithmetic involved in calculating metacentric height (GM), the vertical difference between the centre of gravity and the metacentre which is related to the centre of buoyancy. Fortunately the position of the metacentre will fall as a vessel heels because the effective breadth of the ship increases. Positive stability returns at a certain angle, the angle of loll, and the ship will not capsize. As Tony points out, not a comfortable state of affairs but safe. This angle of loll can be reduced and I recall that the correct procedure for doing this used to be one of the favourite questions asked of candidates for orals for any grade of ticket. Happily, I was never interrogated on this and neither did I have to tackle the problem at sea but I can still remember the answers required. The trick was to lower the ship's centre of gravity and the way to do this was either to fill a double-bottom tank on the low side of the ship or jettison cargo from the high side of the ship. At first glance this seems to be the wrong way round but the answer lies in maximising the righting levers available. But this might entail fouling an empty fuel tank with seawater or losing money or freight so the pragmatic answer was obviously to loll on and give the dockside photographer something to picture on arrival.

I look forward to a future issue of *Record* when some photographs of severely listing vessels will allow the readership to reminisce about rigging shifting boards and the adequacy or otherwise of cargo lashings. Happy days! JOHN GOBLE, 55 Shanklin Road, Southampton SO15 7RG

Good to see *Chapel River* in *Record* 31, though I rather think she is sailing, not out of Blyth where she was built, but from the Tyne, where she received her engines and was completed.

On the topic of ships carrying timber deck cargoes developing lists, on page 192 we read 'This has caused her to become unstable…' As page 103 in *Record* 30 says 'a slight list is a frequent problem when carrying deck cargoes of timber'. But it was not considered a problem by those carrying such cargoes at the time. It was, rather, a normal state of affairs, in which bunkers (bottom weight) were consumed, while rain and seawater coming aboard added top weight. This did not make the ship dangerously unstable. Rather, she lay to the angle of loll which restored her stability because of the now wider waterplane the lolled hull presented. As long as she had no slack tanks (and her people took pains to prevent her fuel and/or water double bottom tanks becoming slack, in other words, not completely full) she was in no danger of flipping over.

Although the loll did nothing for the comfort of those on board, it was often used to discharge part of her cargo on arrival, when the quick-release gear securing the deck cargo lashings was used to enable much of the timber to fall overboard into the dock naturally, to be collected by the consignee timber merchants before the rest of her cargo was unloaded conventionally. Many a ship has part unloaded her cargo of pitprops in this way. Slack tanks *were* the danger of course, and ships have capsized by flipping over - but such disasters were rare.
CAPTAIN A.W. KINGHORN, 15 Kendal Avenue, Cullercoats, North Shields, Tyne & Wear NE30 3AQ

Restoring *Daniel Adamson*

The steam tug/tender *Daniel Adamson* is currently undergoing restoration to bring her back to full working order. Over the years many of her fixtures and fittings have been removed, probably because it was assumed that the vessel was to be scrapped. I would like to appeal to anyone who has or knows the whereabouts of any of her fittings to get in touch with me at the address below or e-mail me at nigel@farrell0000.freeserve.co.uk

The *Daniel Adamson* is a twin screw coal burner built on Merseyside in 1903 and if anyone would like to help preserve this unique vessel or would like more information please contact Patrick Crecraft, Secretary, Daniel Adamson Preservation Society, 8 Newlands, Naseby, Northampton NN6 6DE or e-mail to pat@pcrecraft.freeserve.co.uk or visit our website at www.danieladamson.com
NIGEL FARRELL, 28 Campbell Road, Winton, Eccles, Manchester M30 8LZ

Penleath particulars

I have the following additional information relating to the small Fowey tug *Penleath* (*Record* 31, page 143):
7.1987: Purchased together with her owners and other units of their fleet by United Towing Ltd.

Daniel Adamson has considerable historic significance. Although associated with the Manchester Ship Canal, she was built for the Shropshire Union Canal as *Ralph Brocklebank*. Her primary job was towing barges from Liverpool to the canal company's dock at Ellesmere Port, but she also had passenger accommodation, hence her suitability to act as the Ship Canal tender. She was bought by the MSC in 1922 and renamed *Daniel Adamson* during a 1936 refit. *[J. & M. Clarkson collection]*

In *Record* 31 we made a plea for a post-war view of *Spidola* of 1905, and fortuitously this photograph turned up in a recently-acquired collection. It shows several modifications from the ship as shown in *Record* 31; in particular the aftermost kingposts have gone, the ship has acquired a wheelhouse, and the ventilators ahead of the funnel appear to have been increased in height. Note that the main topmast still appears to lean forwards. *[Ships in Focus collection]*

11.1987: Sold to Dolphin Towing Services (Captain Chris. Merrick and others), Paignton with the intention of renaming *D.T.S. Seal*, but that was not actioned.
1.1988: Arrived for employment at Weymouth.
7.1988: Sold to Fowey Harbour Commissioners and renamed *Penleath*.
BILL SCHELL, 334 South Franklin Street, Holbrook MA 02343, USA

Essex Abbey trials
There seems little doubt that the photograph of *Essex Abbey* on page 174 of *Record* 31 was taken on trials, as she is flying 'A' from her foremast ('I am undertaking speed trials'). It is interesting that she also wears the Scottish flag at her mainmast; I have not seen this before, usually a ship on trials wears the builder's house flag prior to delivery to the owners. Perhaps Greenock and Grangemouth Dockyard Co. Ltd. had not got one, and flew the flag as a patriotic gesture! Very little has been published, as far as I know, about shipbuilders' house flags, could anyone provide an article?
TONY SMYTHE, 35 Avondale Road, Rayleigh, Essex SS6 8NJ
There is a short section on shipbuilders' flags in J.L. Loughran's 'A Survey of Mercantile Houseflags and Funnels' (Waine Research, Albrighton, 1979), but no flag is given for Greenock and Grangemouth. Ed.

Laurence Dunn has kindly submitted this photograph of the *Essex Abbey*, which he took at Fowey in April 1933.

From barques to bottoms
I must take issue with Ross Osmond's statement on page 186 of *Record* 31 that 'a barque at any time only has three masts', which would have come as a real surprise to Ferdinand Laeisz, Gustaf Erikson, and to the publishers of 'Collin's English Dictionary'!

About 20 years ago *Torrington* (*Record* 31, page 167) was displayed in splendid model form at an exhibition featuring tramp steamers of bygone years in the old Cardiff Industrial Museum. According to one of the visitors, she was stopped by the surfaced *U 55* and her crew taken from the lifeboats on to the casing of the submarine, whereupon their hands were tied, no doubt giving the impression that they were to be taken below. In the event they were all drowned when the submarine submerged. I have not heard this account before or since, but have no reason to doubt its veracity.

I saw *Spidola* (page 163) in London's India Docks around 1948, and again in the St. Lawrence river about 1954 when we (unsurprisingly) overtook her in *Alsatia*, with her steering chains clearly visible, clanking along her after deck. An old Latvian seaman told me that the PD monogram was known disparagingly in Riga as 'Pu Dirsa' (my phonetics), translating as 'Blue bottom' (actually, a more colloquial term was used), which is unlikely to be confirmed anywhere in print.
ALAN E. PHIPPS, 2 Riverside Road, Droitwich Spa, Worcestershire WR9 8UW

Roland's repairs
In Captain Kinghorn's article on the *Dunedin Star* (*Record* 9) you noted that in her later years as *Roland* she had acquired an unusual bow profile and, as was suggested, I can confirm that this arose from collision damage. I joined *Roland* shortly after her transfer to Lamport and Holt in 1968 and was making my third trip with her as assistant steward. Signing on at Liverpool on 13th December I could not help realising that this would be my 13th voyage. We sailed the following day for Swansea to load tinplate destined for the canneries at Buenos Aires. Our next port of call was El Ferrol, General Franco's birthplace, where we were to pick up a cargo of salt fish for Recife, Brazil. Approaching the berth here near midnight on the 22nd *Roland* came to grief, hitting the concrete quay almost head on. I was down below at the time and did not witness the incident but the impact was substantial, causing even more

damage to the quay than to the bow. With Christmas just a couple of days away repairs were hurriedly arranged at Lisbon where we were unexpectedly, but delightedly, able to enjoy the festive period ashore. The work of fitting a temporary bow was quickly completed, and we resumed our disrupted voyage on 4th January. This was to be my last voyage with *Roland* and with Lamports - my next berth was with the other half of the family on Holt's *Memnon*.

ALBERT ROONEY, 1 Williams Avenue, Bootle, Merseyside L20 0AT

Lamport's management were no doubt well pleased to have had Roland *returned to service so speedily over the Christmas period but the repairs were not to prove very durable as a subsequent 'Lloyd's Weekly Casualty Report' records. Ten days into her transatlantic crossing the new plating started to detach. Despite the fair weather conditions and a reduction in speed, the repair continued to deteriorate and three days later the bow plating had opened at the seam and had rolled back on both sides. On arrival at Buenos Aires most of the new steelwork was found to have gone leaving just part of one plate welded to the ship's side. Further repairs were effected here, with reinforcing bars and a cement box fitted. Ed*

Barry corrections

Earl of Douglas - owner was Dobbie, not Dobbin.
Glenspean - owner was Gardiner, not Gardner.
Vimeira - Gow, Harrison and Co. were Glasgow based and as far as I am aware registered all their ships there.

As far as the photo captions are concerned:
Page 165 bottom - I suspect this photo dates from rather later than 1900 - most of the steamers look like post-1900 builds - if the names of the two vessels in the foreground can be made out on the original, it should be possible to establish the date with some certainty.
Page 170 top - this *Trevose* is the second not the third of the name.
Page 173 top (caption on 172) - the voyage details are incorrect - *Trongate* was sunk while bound from the Tyne to France with coal.
Page 172 top - Denholm were Greenock-based and used composite one word names (ie *Broompark, Wellpark*); Park was a Glasgow company and used family members' names.
Page 174 top - Strictly speaking, the text is accurate, but the Rio Cape Line Ltd. was a vehicle set up by Furness Withy to take over the entire Gardiner fleet - the latter was already known informally as the Rio Cape Line, although Gardiner did not actually set up a company with that name.

The best part of the whole article for me was the appearance of the *Gracefield* - my grandfather served his apprenticeship on her (I have his letter of reference from the Captain) and would actually have been on board when she was in Barry in September 1913.

Dr MALCOLM COOPER, Flat 5, Leonard Court, 68 Westbourne Terrace, London W2 3UF

Fate of the *Walkure*

The *Walkure* (Record 31, page 169) was captured at Makatea Island on 12th August 1914 by the French gunboat *Zelee*, which was based at Papeete, the capital of Tahiti. In September, *Zelee* was disarmed and her guns landed for the defence of Tahiti.

Papeete was attacked on 22nd September 1914 by the German East Asiatic Squadron consisting of the armoured cruisers (not battle cruisers, as claimed in *Record*) SMS *Scharnhorst* and *Gneisenau* in company with two colliers, all under the command of Vice Admiral Maximilian Graf von Spee. The Squadron had been cruising across the Pacific from its base at Tsingtau in China. They arrived at Bora Bora in the Society Islands on 21st September and, meeting no resistance from the few French inhabitants, coaled and landed men to gather supplies. However, Von Spee needed even more supplies and headed for Papeete, just 150 miles away. When they approached at dawn on 22nd September, the *Scharnhorst* and *Gneisenau* found that the French governor was ready to make a fight of it. The *Zelee* had been scuttled in the entrance to prevent them penetrating the harbour.

The armoured cruisers opened fire on the fort and the *Zelee*, expending irreplaceable ammunition. The French set fire to the coal stocks and blew up their store houses. The leading marks into the harbour had been removed making it too hazardous for the Germans to approach, so that they had to withdraw empty handed. The French then sent a steamer to Samoa with news of the attack, from where it reached London on 30th September.

There is nothing in the accounts I have read on exactly what happened to the *Walkure*, but a reader may know of a French language report on the events at Papeete in 1914 and 1915 that will clear this up.

Referring to *Record* 31, page 188: the Leyland Line's *Kingstonian* was damaged by a torpedo from the German submarine *UB 68* on 11th April 1918 whilst off Sardinia in position 39.20 north by 07.10 east during a voyage from Alexandria to Marseilles with troops and equipment. One life was lost. She was beached in Calaforte Bay, Sardinia and on 29th April 1918, during the salvage operations described in David Astbury's letter, was torpedoed by the German submarine *UB 48*, subsequently becoming a total loss.

DEREK ATHERTON, 3 Twyford Place, Fingerpost, St. Helens, Merseyside WA9 1BN

Dave Hocquard sends this photograph, to follow-up the article on Fowey tugs in *Record* 31, a further view of *Cruden Bay*.

The date is about 1929, and she seems to be taking part in some sort of inspection, probably a jolly for the local harbour commissioners, councillors and whoever else could talk themselves on board. Note the large flag at the main, possibly the houseflag of the Great Western Railway.

Several rakes of railway wagons dedicated to clay traffic line the bank of this china clay exporting harbour. *[Dave Hocquard collection]*

THE DONKEYMAN'S TALE

Ken Garrett

The small steam ship *Springfjord* had a relatively short but rather troubled life and, having survived a major conflict, met her end in a much smaller civil war. She had been ordered by Springwell Shipping Co. Ltd. of London from Trondheims Mekaniske Verksted of Trondheim in Norway as yard number 208. Launched in 1940 she was seized by the advancing German forces and completed to their account as *Rudesheimer* for management by D.D.G. 'Hansa' of Bremen.

In September 1943, when engaged on the Norwegian northern trade, the ship was torpedoed and damaged by the Russian submarine M 104. However, she was brought to safety, repaired and returned to service.

In May 1945 she was taken in prize at Tonsberg and in 1946 renamed *Empire Springfjord* by the Ministry of Transport, London and given to Springwell Shipping to manage. In 1947 she reverted to her original name *Springfjord*. By this time there was a subtle change in her owners who became Springfjord Shipping Co. Ltd. while Springwell Shipping Co. Ltd. remained the managers.

She had a triple-expansion steam engine made by the shipbuilder and there is a possibility that she was originally a coal burner but had been converted to oil fuel at some time, certainly by 1953. As built she was a three-island type with a long bridge deck. However, also by 1953, the short well decks had been built up and she became a flush deck ship. Strangely, her tonnages do not appear to reflect any of these alterations.

My interest and knowledge of this ship began when researching for a book on Comben Longstaff and Co. Ltd. who had managed one of the Springwell ships. I discovered that one of the Longstaff chief engineers, Hugh Tonkin of Newlyn who I knew well, had sailed on a couple of Springwell ships and had an extraordinary story to tell. Given that even in the early 1950s Britain still had such a large merchant fleet it was inevitable that some ships would become embroiled in the problems of other countries. Many merchant seamen of the time had some hair-raising experiences and most survived but few had their ship sunk under them like Hugh.

He joined the ship in Antwerp in March 1953 as the donkeyman and sailed to the USA to pick up a Grace Line charter trading between North, Central and South America. At some stage he was promoted to fourth engineer but it seems that he still carried out the donkeyman's duties. He was responsible for eight steam winches, the windlass and capstan; the winches in particular were hard worked because the cargo was loaded and discharged by ship's gear in every port. Occasionally, one of the pins would jump out of the gooseneck and the derrick heel would crash onto the deck making a fearful noise.

The event took place on 27th June 1954 when the ship was at anchor off San Jose in Guatemala. Hugh had gone below to the boiler room at 06.30 to check the boiler feed water and the pressure for steam on deck. He heard a crash and took it to be one of the derricks jumping the gooseneck and set off to investigate. Walking from the boiler room into the engine room he found paint, oil and water everywhere and behind the engine near the hotwell tank he saw a 500lb bomb with yellow rings painted on it lying on the plates. He ran out of the engine room and found the third engineer, naked, pointing at the remains of his cabin. The bomb had entered through the side of the ship under his bunk, carried it across the room into the alleyway and then went through the bulkhead and into the engine room. Thinking how lucky they had been that there had been nobody else in the engine room - for now a fire had started - he went out on deck.

The captain, Thomas Bradford, was on the boat deck discussing the fire and lowering the lifeboats. Hugh ran around to the port side of the boat deck and saw another 500lb bomb lying on the skylight. It had struck and damaged the boat davit making it impossible to lower the port side boat.

At this point he saw an aeroplane coming in for a second attack. Looking round he saw the radio officer and one of the sailors standing by the after hatch watching the plane and, running across, he threw them to the deck. A bomb went into the hold and exploded sending hatch boards

Springfjord, still with a long bridge deck. *[J.& M. Clarkson*

and cargo into the air. Looking up, Hugh saw the ship's dog and cat running at full speed along the deck and straight over the stern, the cat was running under the dog's belly as if for protection.

The plane came in again and dropped a bomb in the forward hold sending cargo into the air and starting another fire. He thought it was the same plane but later wondered whether it had been two. The plane had no markings and Hugh was pretty sure that it was a Lockheed Lightning (P-38) because he had seen them as a boy at RAF Predannack in Cornwall. However, the press referred to the attacker as a Republic Thunderbolt (P-47). Later information confirms that it was a single Lockheed Lightning piloted by an American, Ferdinand Schoup. Co-incidentally, the aeroplane is now preserved at the Seattle Museum of Flight.

The ship's safety equipment was in a bad state. It was not possible to get into the engine room to start a pump and the emergency diesel pump had been sabotaged by a crew member discharged earlier for disciplinary reasons. But in any case the hoses were either missing or rotten and nobody could remember having a fire or boat drill for months.

Eventually they managed to lower the starboard side boat and pull clear while a motor launch from ashore took off the captain, his wife and the American super-cargo. The captain suggested that they row to neighbouring El Salvador to get away from the revolution but they chose to make for the nearest shore and even then the boat was sinking by the time they arrived. Despite everything that had occurred there were no casualties.

The local people made them welcome and put them up in beach houses for the night. Soldiers of the Guatemalan army stood guard. The ship was still burning but the captain asked for volunteers to return aboard to see if anything could be done. Hugh declined: he had had quite enough for one day. There were only three real English speakers: the captain, the radio officer and Hugh and the crew used him as an interpreter to find out from the captain what was happening. By this time he had befriended the chief engineer who was a former U-boat engineer.

The ship sank some days later and, walking along the beach in the morning, they found the bodies of the cat and dog. Later, a bus arrived to take them to Guatemala City with an army escort. People along the way were very friendly and gave them clothes, soap and other necessities.

The President of Guatemala went on the radio to say how much the crew had helped the country and thanked them for everything. Unfortunately, he disappeared the following day and attitudes changed immediately. The people were naturally frightened and unsure of their fate when the rebels arrived.

The next day Hugh and the chief engineer walked into town and watched the rebels take over the Presidential Palace. On their way back they noticed two official-looking cars pulled up outside the Guatemala Hotel where they were staying. The two debated whether to go in or to cut and run but, realistically, they had nowhere else to go so they put on brave faces and went in. They were met by a number of soldiers who, at gunpoint, ordered them into the bar with the rest of the crew to drink to their victory. One could see straight away that these soldiers were not particularly worldly-wise for it is indeed a rare occasion that British seamen, or seamen from anywhere for that matter, need to be forced at gunpoint into a bar for a drink. So they all had a good afternoon and then the soldiers left. Shortly afterwards, the hotel manager came to the captain with the bill for all the drinks. He was not amused.

The plight of the survivors was taken up by the Foreign Office in London and the Minister of State, Mr Selwyn Lloyd, said in the House of Commons that British representatives in neighbouring states had been instructed to make urgent enquiries to find the nationality of the attacker. On arriving home they were briefed not to make any comments about the attack. Hugh was asked to go on the BBC programme 'In Town Tonight' but had to decline.

On a happier note, Hugh's marriage to his fiancée Patricia Bowman was now able to take place. The wedding had been postponed on a couple of occasions because he could not get leave. It is an ill wind that does nobody any good and that sinister aircraft certainly pre-empted things in a dramatic way.

The foregoing is mainly based on Hugh's recollection of events but subsequently some background information has come my way from America. It must be remembered that the mid-1950s was a period of tension and anti-communist hysteria in America where the fear of 'reds under the bed' was real. The US Central Intelligence Agency (CIA) was closely watching the development of left wing revolutionary governments anywhere in the world but particularly in Central and South America. The government of Guatemala led by Colonel Arbenz, because it had initiated some social and economic reforms, was considered a threat and a covert operation was set up by the CIA with the code name PB Success. Colonel Castillo Armas was identified as a suitable successor and funds were provided to de-stabilise the government and through a coup establish an administration led by Castillo Armas which would be more friendly to the US.

The *Springfjord* sailed innocently into this situation when she arrived at San Jose in June 1954. Such political scenarios naturally spawn a number of rumours and the President of nearby Nicaragua, Anastasio Somoza, was informed by his intelligence sources that the ship was carrying crated aircraft, arms and ammunition to re-arm the Guatemalan army. This could have stalled the CIA operation and also have had a knock-on affect on Somoza's hold on power in his own country. The American in charge of PB Success refused permission for an air strike on the ship but in a confused situation was overruled by President Somoza who ordered them to sink the ship.

Ferdinand Schoup, a former USAF pilot but now flying for the Liberation Air Force, was instructed to carry out the order. When he arrived at the secret airfield, Schoup found that the only operational Thunderbolt (P-47) was elsewhere and the others were grounded. However, there was a Lightning (P-38), repaired after a recent forced landing, that was considered to be airworthy. This report goes on to state that Schoup dropped leaflets on the ship warning them he was going to attack before making another pass and dropping two bombs. This is slightly at odds with Hugh's version of events because he mentions four bombs, the first two of which did not explode. A possible explanation is that Hugh mistook the first two for containers of some sort with the leaflets, or maybe they were in the nature of a 'shot across the bows' by the pilot who perhaps knew they were not armed. Whatever the true facts of the matter, it is clear that Schoup had a good aim and achieved the required hits although the ship did not sink for several days.

The rumours about her cargo were proved to be false and the ship was carrying nothing more lethal than coffee, sugar and cotton. Naturally the underwriters of ship and cargo became very interested and the British government lodged complaints about the wanton and illegal act. To calm things down the CIA put the new President Castillo Armas in funds and instructed him to offer the British compensation of $900,000. He was to make it clear that his government was in a poor financial state and that this sum represented a great sacrifice and was a gesture of friendship. More was eventually forthcoming but the CIA was on the horns of a dilemma because to increase their donation to the Guatemalans to the point of satisfying all the demands and heading off any awkward investigations would probably have declared their hand.

Top: The fast reefer *Thorstrand* (1) was sunk in 1943. *[B. & A. Feilden/J. & M. Clarkson]*

Middle: *Thorscape* (1) was launched in 1920 but only completed in 1941. Seen here at Cape Town in 1948. *[F.W. Hawks collection]*

Right: Also at Cape Town, *Thor 1* (2) was built for the Pacific Islands Transport Line in 1938. *[Andrew Ingpen collection]*

Opposite page: Many Thor Dahl ships featured this bow badge of the Norse god Thor, an obvious reference to Thor Dahl's name. Surrounded by bolts of lightening, Thor clutches his trade mark hammer. At his feet are symbols of the sealing and whaling activities of the company. Two seals are on either side whilst he stands on a circular motif with a whale in the shape of the letter C for Christensen. One of the six-pointed stars above the badge is also to be found fore and aft on the white band of the funnel. *[Robert Pabst]*

THE WHITE FLEET OF THOR DAHL

Peter Newall

For much of the 20th century the Norwegian firm Thor Dahl was known mainly for its interests in whaling and oil. It also owned a very interesting fleet of reefers and general cargo ships which are the prime focus of this article.

The Christensen family from Sandefjord in Norway had been pioneers in whaling. In 1903 Christen Christensen (1845-1923) founded AS Ørnen and in 1905 sent the first whale factory ship *Admiralen* (1,517/1869) to the Antarctic. The family-owned Framnæs shipyard also built many sealing and whaling vessels whilst Christen Christensen's son Lars (1884-1965) married the daughter of another well-known whaling ship owner Thor Dahl (1862-1920). Dahl formed Bryde & Dahls Hvalfangerselskab (whaling company) A/S in 1910 with his first ship *Thor I* (4,353/1890), a former British cargo ship - see *Record* 5, page 37.

After the death of his father-in-law, Lars Christensen took charge of the commercial interests of A/S Thor Dahl and merged those with his own. A/S Thor Dahl also later became managers of the various constituent parts of the company, including Bryde & Dahls Hvalfangerselskab A/S, and A/S Ørnen. By the late 1930s A/S Thor Dahl had become a major whaling and tanker company. However, with increasing international pressure to control the number of whales slaughtered each year, Lars Christensen decided to diversify into the reefer and dry cargo trades.

In 1937 and 1938 a pair of 15-knot, 3,000gt reefers were completed for the company. *Scebeli* was built at Copenhagen by Burmeister & Wain and was give an Italian name because of a 22-month charter to an Italian company, which was cancelled in September 1937. *Thorstrand*, on the other hand, came from the Framnæs yard and was used in a joint venture with Fred. Olsen, apparently carrying fruit from the west coast of the United States to Europe. Both reefers were used on this service until the outbreak of war. After the occupation of Norway in 1940, an organisation called The Norwegian Shipping and Trade Mission, usually referred to as Nortraship, was set up to oversee the management of Norwegian shipping. In the spring of 1942 both *Scebeli* and *Thorstrand* (1) were required to move from the relative safety of the US and South American trades to the vital transatlantic supply routes. Unfortunately, German submarines sank both ships less than seven weeks apart in 1943.

Meanwhile, in 1938, the Pacific Islands Transport Line was founded to operate a new service between the US west coast and the islands of the Pacific and Polynesia. Norwegian shipping lines had long been associated with the Pacific trades, although most were based in the Far East. Framnæs built the 2,500gt motorship *Thor I* (2) for this service. She was a unique-looking ship with a long bridge deck, short wells fore and aft, and tall masts and derrick posts which were essential for working cargo over the side. In 1940, she too came under the management of Nortraship.

Like many Norwegian shipowners, Lars Christensen went into exile in 1940. His main base during the war years was New York where he had a suite in the Waldorf Astoria Hotel. He remained active in the shipping business especially with his interests in the Pacific and the Frango Corporation. The latter had been formed in 1940 to take over the US-registered American Whaling Company founded in the 1930s by Christensen so that whale oil could be imported into the US tax-free. Its whale factory ship *Frango*, which had also been managed by Thor Dahl, was renamed *Clifford* and sold to Japan in 1941. In 1940 the Frango Corporation bought the semi-completed hull of a cargo ship launched for Italian interests in 1920. This vessel was completed as *Philae* in April 1941. The Frango Corporation, registered in Panama, was presumably set up to avoid this vessel and *Frango* coming under Nortraship control. After the war, *Philae* was re-engined and was bought by Thor Dahl in 1948 and renamed *Thorscape* (1) for a new venture between Canada and South Africa.

A regular cargo service between Canada and South Africa had been run by Elder Dempster since 1901. The first ships on the service were *Melville* (4,439/1902) and *Monarch* (7,296/1897) and in 1904 they were joined by the unusually named 4,286gt freighter *Canada Cape*. Between 1921 and 1924, four 7,200gt Clyde-built sisters were completed for the run. Named after towns in Canada, *Calgary*, *Cochrane*, *Calumet* and *Cariboo* also had accommodation for eight first class passengers and stopped in West Africa on both legs of the journey. *Cariboo* was wrecked off the coast of South Africa in 1928 and her place was taken by the motorship *Ediba* (6,919/1923), which was renamed *Mattawin*. The three C-ships survived the war and in 1945 Elder Dempster Lines (Canada) Ltd. was formed primarily to purchase and operate, under the Canadian flag, five 7,000gt Canadian-built *Park* standard ships on the Canada-South Africa service. These were renamed *Cabano*, *Cambray*, *Cargill*, *Chandler* and *Cottrell*. Although the service, which ran between Canada and South and East African ports, was profitable, a shortage of foreign currency in South Africa and strikes led to a reduction in cargoes and a gradual withdrawal from the route which came to an end in July 1950.

In 1947 Lars Christensen was approached by New York shipowner Alfred Clegg of the Kerr Steamship Company Inc. Clegg suggested that Thor Dahl start up a line, based at Montreal, between Canada and South Africa and that the general agents in Canada and Africa would be provided by the Kerr organisation. Christensen already had sealing interests in Canada and in April the following year, Christensen Canadian South African Lines was formed. The chartered Danish vessel *Norden* (4,685/1946) took the first monthly sailing from Montreal in May 1948. She was followed by another charter, the Norwegian Liberty ship

Thorstrand (2) was the second of three Burntisland-built ships completed in 1948 and 1949. *[Andrew Ingpen collection]*

Valhall (7,221/1943) and the first of the Thor-owned ships on the service, *Thorscape*.

In order to operate a regular monthly service, three 3,700gt cargo ships were ordered from the Scottish shipyard, Burntisland. *Thorshall*, *Thorstrand* (2) and *Thorsisle* (1) were delivered in quick succession between November 1948 and June 1949. This trio also had comfortable accommodation for 12 passengers which included a large promenade space plus a lounge and dining saloon overlooking the fore deck. With their arrival, *Thorscape* (1) was transferred to the Pacific Islands Transport Line but was sold in 1950.

The success of the line soon saw the ports of call extended to East Africa, and Holland-Afrika Lijn was appointed the general agent for all African ports whilst Kerr Steamships (Canada) Ltd. continued to be responsible for the Canadian end of the route. The name Christensen Canadian South African Lines was also changed to Christensen Canadian African Lines. Three larger and faster ships with split superstructures were ordered from Bergens Mek.

Værksted and these ships, *Thorsgaard*, *Thorscape* (2) and *Thor I* (3), eventually replaced the Burntisland trio. They were also followed between 1958 and 1960 by a similar but more powerful set of three ships, *Thorshope* (1), *Thorsriver* and *Thorstream*, this time from the Dahl-owned Framnæs shipyard. *Thorstream* was also probably one of the last cargo ships built with split midships superstructure.

Following the advent of the new vessels, *Thorsisle* was placed on the Pacific Islands Transport Line whilst *Thorshall* was used on the Norse Oriental Line, a 50:50 joint venture with Bruusgaard, Kiøsterud and Co., Drammen. This started in October 1954 between Sydney, Brisbane, Townsville, Djakarta, Singapore and Penang. Bruusgaard withdrew from the deal in 1957 and the place of its ship was taken by *Thorstrand* (2). The second *Thorscape* replaced *Thorshall* in 1961 whilst a 1951-built second-hand ship was bought in 1964 and renamed *Thorsorient* to take over from *Thorstrand*. With the sale of *Thorsorient* and *Thorscape* (2) in the mid 1970s, the service closed.

Always in immaculate condition, *Thor I* (3) and her split-superstructure sisters were amongst the most attractive cargo ships trading to South Africa in the 1950s and 1960s. *[Ian Shiffman]*

Meanwhile, in 1956 and 1959, two freighters of almost 9,000gt were added to the fleet, the German-built *Thorsdrake* and the Swedish-built *Thorscarrier*. These were used mainly as tramps but also as additional ships on the Canada-Africa run. Between 1964 and 1968 Framnæs also built three fast reefers for the company, *Thorsdrott*, *Thorsøy* and *Thorstind*. In the 1970s this trio was sold to another Norwegian firm, Sigurd Haavik A/S of Haugesund. They were also the last of the conventional cargo ships with engines amidships built for Thor Dahl.

In the Pacific, *Thorsgaard* and *Thor I* (3) were transferred to the Pacific Islands Transport Line and another *Thorsisle* joined the fleet in 1970. The last-mentioned was a former Fred. Olsen ship, *Bonanza* and, after her sale in 1975, the route between San Francisco, Tahiti, Samoa, Fiji, New Caledonia and New Guinea was operated with chartered tonnage. Although it closed in 1985, it was resumed in July 1990 following the acquisition of the South Sea Steamship Company of San Francisco and its chartered ship *Moana Pacific* which was bought by Thor Dahl in 1993 and sold three years later with a three-year charter back. In July 1998, the line was bought by Hamburg Süd.

Much of the cargo from Canada to Africa was paper, newsprint and other forestry products. The return cargoes were often coffee, tea, sisal and other general cargoes. In the 1960s, however, Christensen Canadian African Lines started carrying oranges and deciduous fruit from South Africa. During this period the Framnæs trio *Thorshope* (1), *Thorsriver* (1) and *Thorstream*, were fitted with refrigerated compartments and given flush 'tween deck hatches for forklift handling of cargo. The company also ordered its first engines aft ship on the route, *Thorswave*, which was completed in 1968. She was later given a set of Stülcken masts.

In 1977 and 1978, the Framnæs trio were replaced by two multi-purpose ships built in Japan. Capable of carrying 400 TEUs as well as fruit and a wide variety of other cargoes, *Thorscape* (3) and *Thor I* (4) were also the last ships ordered for Christensen Canadian African Lines. They became the proverbial workhorses on the route for over twenty years. The 1980s were a particularly difficult time with sanctions being imposed on South Africa and with falling loads from East Africa, the service generally terminated in Durban. To reduce costs *Thorscape* (3) and *Thor I* (4) were 'sold' to a Thor Dahl subsidiary in 1986 and chartered back with Norwegian officers and Indian crew.

Business picked up during the post-Apartheid era and in 1996 a Singapore company bought *Thorscape* (3) and *Thor I* (4) and leased them back on charter. In the late 1990s, they were joined briefly by three chartered Russian-built ro-ros, which were renamed *Thorsriver* (2), *Thorshope* (2) and

Thorsdrake at Venice. *[J. & M. Clarkson collection]*

Above: The reefer *Thorsøy*. *[A. Duncan/Ships in Focus collection]*
Below: *Thor I* (4). *[A. Duncan/Ships in Focus collection]*

Thorslake. However, on 31st August 2000 CP Ships acquired Christensen Canadian African Lines and the three chartered ro-ros continued to operate briefly under Lykes names. Although the Thor name is no longer seen along the South African coast, Thor Dahl Shipping remains a major force in shipping with the focus of its operation in container ships. The great god of thunder also continues to have a Dahl presence this year when two 23,761gt, 1989-built, Singapore-owned container ships *HSH Kusu* and *HSH Ubin* were renamed respectively *Thorsriver* and *Thorstream*.

FLEET LIST

SCEBELI 1937-1943 Reefer trades.
3,025g 2,070n 324.3 x 45.8 x 26.1 feet.
Oil engine 9-cyl. 2SCSA by A/S
Burmeister & Wain, Copenhagen; 606
NHP, 15 knots.
2.1937: Completed by A/S Burmeister &
Wain, Copenhagen (Yard No. 630) for
Skibs A/S Thorsholm (A/S Thor Dahl,
managers), Sandefjord as SCEBELI.
21.4.1943: Torpedoed and sunk by the
German submarine U 161 in position
56.07 north by 44.26 west whilst on a
voyage from Liverpool to New York in
ballast. Two men were killed.

THORSTRAND (1) **1938-1943** Reefer
trades.
3,041g 2,070n 321.6 x 46.2 x 26.1 feet.
Oil engine 7-cyl. 2SCSA by Sulzer
Brothers, Winterthur; 775 NHP, 15 knots.
4.1938: Completed by Framnæs Mek.
Værks A/S, Sandefjord (Yard No. 118) for
Skibs A/S Thorsholm (A/S Thor Dahl,
managers), Sandefjord as
THORSTRAND.
6.3.1943: Torpedoed and sunk by the
German submarine U 172 in position
41.23 north by 42.59 west whilst on a
voyage from Liverpool to St. John, New
Brunswick with general cargo and mail.
Four men were killed.

THOR I (2) **1938-1953** Pacific Islands
Transport Line.
2,502g 1,482n 312.7 x 46.7 x 18.5 feet.
Oil engine 6-cyl. 2SCSA by Sulzer
Brothers, Winterthur; 1,500 BHP, 11
knots.

Scebeli.

11.1938: Completed by Framnæs Mek.
Værks A/S, Sandefjord (Yard No.122) for
Bryde & Dahls Hvalfangerselskab A/S
(A/S Thor Dahl, managers), Sandefjord as
THOR I.
4.1940-9.1945: Under Nortraship
management.
10.1950: Transferred to A/S Thor Dahls
Hvalfangerselskab (A/S Thor Dahl,
managers), Sandefjord.
12.1953: Sold to Skibs A/S Vilhelm
Torkildsen Rederi, Bergen and renamed
MARSTENEN.
10.1957: Sold to Rederi A/B Kullaberg
(Karl Axel Sjøsten, managers), Höganäs
and renamed HEDERA.
11963: Sold at auction to Rederiet for m.s.
'Skandinav' (L.E. Påhlsson, manager),
Helsingborg (nominee for Skandinaviska
Banken) and renamed SKANDINAV.

9.1963: Sold to Dimitiros Coustas and
Nicolaos Grigoriou, Piraeus and renamed
FANI.
1.9.1969: Beached on Salamis Island after
a fire broke out while under repair at
Piraeus.
27.9.1969: Arrived Eleusis for demolition
by B.E.M.

THORSCAPE (1) **1948-1949**
Christensen Canadian South African Line;
1949-1950 Pacific Islands Transport Line.
4,402g 3,245n 370.0 x 52.2 x 24.7 feet.
4.1941: Two oil engines 9-cyl. 4SCSA
built in 1932 by New London S. & E. Co.,
New London, Connecticut; 436 NHP.
5.1946: Two oil engines 8-cyl. 4SA
geared by Enterprise Engineering and
Foundry Company, San Francisco;
2,400BHP, 10 knots

Thor 1 (2) at Cape Town in October 1952. *[A. Duncan/Ships in Focus collection]*

Thorscape (1) at Cape Town. August 1950. *[A. Duncan/Ships in Focus collection]*

1920: Launched by International Shipbuilding Company, Pascagoula, Mississippi (Yard No. 2) for Italian interests as TRENTO but not completed.
4.1941: Completed for Frango Corporation, Panama (Lars Christensen, New York, manager) as PHILAE.
5.1946: Re-engined.
6.1948: Sold to Bryde & Dahls Hvalfangerselskab A/S (A/S Thor Dahl, managers), Sandefjord and renamed THORSCAPE.
61948: Maiden voyage from Montreal to South Africa for Christensen Canadian South African Line.
10.1950: Sold to Skibs A/S Activa & D/S A/S Ledaal (Brødrene Olsen, managers), Stavanger and renamed LEDAAL.
10.1953: Sold to Montemar S.A. Comercial y Maritima, Montevideo and renamed SUDELMAR.
15.2.1974: Arrived at Bilbao for demolition by Hierros Ardes SA.

THORSHALL 1948-1957 Christensen Canadian South Africa Line later known as Christensen Canadian Africa Line; **1957-1960** Norse Oriental Line.
3,676g 2,040n 387' 6" x 53' 6" x 23' 8"
Oil engine 4-cyl. 2SA by Hawthorn, Leslie and Co. Ltd., Newcastle-upon-Tyne; 4,400 BHP, 14.5 knots.
11.1948: Completed by Burntisland Shipbuilding Co. Ltd., Burntisland (Yard No. 319) for Bryde & Dahls Hvalfangerselskab A/S (A/S Thor Dahl, managers), Sandefjord as THORSHALL.

Thorshall at Cape Town, May 1950. *[A. Duncan/Ships in Focus collection]*

10.1950: Transferred to A/S Thor Dahls Hvalfangerselskab (A/S Thor Dahl, managers).
1.1960: Sold to Poseidon Schiffahrt G.m.b.H., Hamburg and renamed TRANSAMERICA.
1967: Sold to Emma Navigation Corporation, Panama (Methenitis Brothers Shipbrokers, Piraeus) and renamed EMMA METHENITIS under the Greek flag.
1974: Sold to Northway Navigation Corporation, Monrovia (D. Lecanides, Piraeus) and renamed PANTIN under the Greek flag.
1977: Transferred to Alikampos Lines Co. Ltd., Limassol (D. Lecanides, Piraeus) and renamed PANODI.

1977: Sold to Vagal Marine Co. Ltd., Limassol (Maritime Overseas Shipping Co. Ltd. (D.J. Kontogiannis), Piraeus) and renamed ARISTOTELIS.
About 9.3.1978: Arrived at Gadani Beach, Pakistan for demolition.

THORSTRAND (2) **1949-1955**
Christensen Canadian South Africa Line later known as Christensen Canadian Africa Line; **1955-1961** Norse Oriental Line.
3,712g 2,070n 387' 6" x 53' 6" x 23' 8"
Oil engine 4-cyl. 2SA by Hawthorn, Leslie and Co. Ltd., Newcastle-upon-Tyne; 4,400 BHP, 14.5 knots.
4.1949: Completed by Burntisland Shipbuilding Co. Ltd., Burntisland (Yard

Thorstrand in August 1950. *[A. Duncan/Ships in Focus collection]*

No. 320) for Bryde & Dahls
Hvalfangerselskab (A/S Thor Dahl,
managers), Sandefjord as
THORSTRAND.
10.1950: Transferred to A/S Thor Dahls
Hvalfangerselskab (A/S Thor Dahl,
managers), Sandefjord.
1961: Sold to Poseidon Schiffahrt
G.m.b.H., Hamburg and renamed
TRANSEUROPA.
1969: Sold to Floritaram Compania
Navegacion S.A., Panama (Demetrios G.
Ventouris, Piraeus) and renamed
FLORITA under the Greek flag.
3.5.1978: Arrived at Gadani Beach,
Pakistan for demolition.

THORSISLE (1) **1949-1952** Christensen
Canadian South Africa Line later known
as Christensen Canadian Africa Line;
1952-1966 Pacific Islands Transport Line.
3,713g 2,068n 387' 6" x 53' 6" x 23' 8"
Oil engine 4-cyl. 2SA by Hawthorn,
Leslie and Co. Ltd., Newcastle-upon-
Tyne; 4,400 BHP, 14.5 knots.
6.1949: Completed by Burntisland
Shipbuilding Co. Ltd., Burntisland (Yard
No. 321) for Bryde & Dahls
Hvalfangerselskab A/S (A/S Thor Dahl,
managers), Sandefjord as THORSISLE.
10.1950: Transferred to A/S Thor Dahls
Hvalfangerselskab (A/S Thor Dahl,
managers).
8.1966: Sold to Hanseatische Reederi
Emil Offen & Co., Hamburg and renamed
HEIN HOYER.
1969: Sold to Dinaco Compania de
Navegacion S.A., Panama (Methenitis

Thorsisle. [A. Duncan/Ships in Focus collection]

Brothers Shipbrokers, Piraeus) and
renamed DIMITRI METHENITIS under
the Greek flag.
1975: Sold to Massitos Shipping Co. S.A.,
Panama (J.G. Kapranis, Piraeus) and
renamed GEORGIOS K.
1980: Sold to Matara Navigation Co. Ltd.,
Panama (A. Matarangas, Piraeus) and
renamed IOS under the Greek flag.
26.12.1980: Arrived at Gadani Beach,
Pakistan under Panama flag for
demolition.

THORSGAARD 1952-19— Christensen
Canadian Africa Line; **19— -1972** Pacific
Islands Transport Line.
5,077g 2,754n 441' 9" x 58' 2" x 25' 1"
Oil engine 8-cyl. 2SCSA by Sulzer
Brothers, Winterthur; 5,600 BHP, 15
knots.
3.1952: Completed by Bergens Mek.
Værks A/S, Bergen (Yard No. 389) for A/
S Thor Dahls Hvalfangerselskab (AS Thor
Dahl, managers), Sandefjord as
THORSGAARD.

Thorsgaard, at Cape Town, March 1953. *[A. Duncan/Ships in Focus collection]*

3.1972: Sold to Solstads Rederi A/S
(Johannes Solstad), Skudeneshavn and
renamed SOLSYN.
1976: Sold to Montemar S.A. Comercial y
Maritima, Montevideo and renamed
SUDELMAR II.
20.8.1983: Arrived at Bruges for
demolition by Brugse Scheepssloperij.

THORSCAPE (2) **1954-1961**
Christensen Canadian Africa Line; **1961-
1976** Norse Oriental Line.
4,981g 2,755n 442' 0" x 58' 2" x 25' 3"
Oil engine 8-cyl. 2SA by Sulzer Brothers,
Winterthur; 5,600 BHP, 15 knots.
10.1954: Completed by Bergens Mek.
Værks A/S, Bergen (Yard No. 398) for
Skibs AS Thorsholm (A/S Thor Dahl,
managers), Sandefjord as THORSCAPE.
1961: Transferred to A/S Ørnen (A/S Thor
Dahl, managers), Sandefjord.
2.1976: Sold to Pacific International Lines
Pte Ltd, Singapore and renamed KOTA
SABAS.
9.2.1983: Arrived at Sachana, India for
demolition by Metal Scrap Trade Corp.

THOR I (3) **1955-19—** Christensen
Canadian Africa Line; **19— -1973** Pacific
Islands Transport Line.
4,993g 2,773n 442' 3" x 58' 2" x 25' 3"
Oil engine 8-cyl. 2SA by Sulzer Brothers,
Winterthur; 5,600 BHP, 15 knots
11.1955: Completed by Bergens Mek.
Værks A/S, Bergen (Yard No. 403) for
A/S Thor Dahls Hvalfangerselskab (A/S
Thor Dahl, managers), Sandefjord as
THOR I.
4.1973: Sold to Mutual Shipping Co. Ltd.,
Monrovia (Interocean Shipping Co. Ltd.,

Thorscape. [A. Duncan/Ships in Focus collection]

Hong Kong) and renamed SEA CONCORD
under the Panama flag.
19.12.1978: Arrived at Hong Kong for
demolition by Lee Sing and Co. Ltd.

THORSDRAKE 1956-1967 Tramping and
Christensen Canadian Africa Line.
8,924g 5,111n 478' 1" x 61' 10" x 30' 0"
Oil engine 9-cyl. 2SA by MAN, Augsburg;
6,000 BHP, 14 knots.
5.1956: Completed by Lübecker Flender-Werke
A.G., Lübeck (Yard No. 465) for A/S Thor
Dahls Hvalfangerselskab (A/S Thor Dahl,
managers), Sandefjord as THORSDRAKE

1967: Sold to China Ocean Shipping
Company, Shanghai and renamed
NANTONG.
1967: Transferred to Chinese-Tanzanian
Joint Shipping Company, Dar-es-Salaam
and renamed USHIRIKA.
1983: Ownership reverted to China Ocean
Shipping Company, Shanghai and
renamed MING XING.
Late 1980s: Transferred to Shanghai Hai
Xing Shipping Co. Ltd., Shanghai.
12.1989: Last recorded movement outside
China, presumed scrapped.

Thorshope (1). [Ian Shiffman]

THORSHOPE (1) **1958-1978**
Christensen Canadian Africa Line.
5,576g 3,148n 479' 2" x 61' 2" x 26' 6"
Oil engine 6-cyl. 2SA by Sulzer Brothers,
Winterthur; 7,800 BHP, 17 knots.
7.1958: Completed by Framnæs Mek.
Værks A/S, Sandefjord (Yard No. 158) for
A/S Thor Dahls Hvalfangerselskab (A/S
Thor Dahl, managers), Sandefjord as
THORSHOPE.
1961: Transferred to A/S Ørnen (A/S Thor
Dahl, managers), Sandefjord.
1960s: Refrigerated chambers installed for
fruit.
Late 1960s: Flush hatches on main deck
fitted by Framnæs Mek. Værks A/S,
Sandefjord.
1978: Sold to Ocean Tramping Co. Ltd.,
Hong Kong and then on to China Ocean

Shipping Company, Shanghai and renamed
LIU PAN SHAN.
29.12.1980: Arrived Gadani Beach,
Pakistan for demolition.

THORSCARRIER 1959-1968
Tramping and Christensen Canadian
Africa Line.
8,742g 4,907n 467' 11" x 61' 0" x 29' 8"
Götaverken-type oil engine 7-cyl. 2SA by
Uddevallavarvet A/B, Uddevalla; 6,550
BHP, 15 knots.
28.4.1959: Launched by Uddevallavarvet
A/B, Uddevalla (Yard No. 174) for A/S
Odd & A/S Ørnen (A/S Thor Dahl,
managers), Sandefjord as
THORSCARRIER.
7.1959: Completed.

11.1968: Sold to Skips-A/S
Malmstransport (Den Norske Amerikalinje
A/S, managers), Olso and renamed
VINDAFJORD.
2.1973: Transferred to Den Norske
Amerikalinje A/S, Olso.
10.1978: Sold to Frijoles Compania
Naviera S.A. (Diana Shipping Agencies
S.A., managers), Piraeus and renamed
NORDAVE.
21.6.1979: Stranded during monsoon in
position 24.14 north by 67.16 east whilst on
a voyage from Karachi to Kandla in ballast.
Later declared a constructive total loss.
1980: Sold to Pakistani shipbreakers.

[*To be concluded in* Record 33]

Thorscarrier. [Peter Newall]

AMERICAN STANDARDS

Paul Boot

Formed on 26th October 1936 under the mandate of the Merchant Marine Act, the United States Maritime Commission was charged with rejuvenating America's merchant fleet. The initial programme inaugurated the following year called for the construction of 50 ships per annum over a ten-year period but as the international situation deteriorated the schedule was doubled each year and by 1941 had risen to 400 ships per annum. By this time the remit had widened to include ships for the US Navy, with many of the cargo ship hulls being adapted for a variety of auxiliary roles. To meet this ever increasing demand existing shipyards were expanded and new yards established. Construction times were drastically reduced by the greater use of prefabrication and welding, pushing these techniques to, and often beyond, their limits. With the United States drawn into the conflict in December 1941 the need for new ships had taken on an even more urgent dimension and under a separate emergency programme over 3,700 vessels were built in addition to the 2,918 ships that were ultimately authorised under the original long term programme.

As peace returned this vast armada became available for the task it had originally been conceived. United States companies avidly rebuilt their fleets with these fast modern ships and, well into the post-war years, most were substantially if not entirely comprised of these standard designs. But there were far more ships than even the United States could trade commercially and those which were surplus to requirements were offered for sale to foreign countries. Both liner companies and flag-of-convenience operators eagerly acquired large numbers of all the types but in particular the cheaper 'Emergency' designs. Well into the early 1960s these ships were still a familiar sight around the world and in this portfolio we look first at a selection of the cargo ships completed under the Maritime Commission's original programme.

One of United States Lines' many C2-S-B1 type turbine steamers, *American Producer* (8,433/1943) provides an impressive and appropriately named reminder of this gargantuan feat of shipbuilding. Completed as the naval transport *Ormsby* by Moore Dry Dock Co., she was scrapped at Kaohsiung in July 1969 *[Roy Kittle collection]*

DINGALAN BAY
Pennsylvania Shipyards Inc., Beaumont; 1942, 5,185g, 412 feet
Two oil engines 2SCSA 6-cyl. by Nordberg Manufacturing Company, Milwaukee geared to a single shaft; 4,150 BHP
The C1 type ships were the smallest of the three original designs produced by the Commission and encompassed four main variants: shelter-deck (C1-A) and full scantling (C1-B) types, with each having both steam- and motor-engined versions. *Cape St. Elias* was one of several C1-A motorships that were sold to Norwegian owners becoming first *Bowrio* and later *Nopal Branco*. Acquired by the Philippine based Universal Shipping Lines Inc., in 1967, *Dingalen Bay* was sold for breaking in September 1973 as the last of the C1 types were reaching the end of their days. *[David Salisbury]*

FLYING SPRAY
The Pusey & Jones Corporation, Wilmington, Delaware; 1944, 5,092g, 394 feet
Two steam turbines, double-reduction geared to a single shaft by Westinghouse Electrical and Manufacturing Company, Pittsburgh, Pennsylvania.
Cape Nome was one of two C1-A types bought by Isbrandtsen Co. Inc. from the grandly titled Ocean Steam Ship Company of Savannah in 1951 who had operated her without change of name since 1947. As *Flying Spray* she ran until 1968 although her funnel markings were changed following the merger of Isbrandtsen with American Export Lines in 1960. Her new Australian owners placed her under the Panamanian flag as *Tia Pepita* but two years later she was broken up at Hong Kong.
Isbrandtsen operated five C1s and in the final days of December 1951 their *Flying Enterprise* (6,714/1944) came to the world's attention as heroic efforts were made to save her as she slowly foundered in the Western Approaches. *[Roy Kittle collection]*

CAPE MARTIN
Consolidated Steel Corporation, Wilmington, California; 1944, 6,724g, 418 feet
Two steam turbines double-reduction geared to a single shaft by Joshua Hendy Iron Works, Sunnyvale.
Of the 173 C1 ships built, 95 were of the C1-B type with all but ten of these powered by steam turbines. Whilst most went into commercial service after the war, over 30 were placed in reserve with the United States Department of Commerce taking responsibility for them after 1950. Still wearing her faded naval colours *Cape Martin* languished at Suisan Bay near San Francisco until April 1975 when she was moved to Richmond for scrapping. *[Roy Kittle collection]*

SERENE MED
South Eastern Shipbuilding Corporation, Savannah; 1946, 3,921g 339 feet
Oil engine 2SCSA 6-cyl. by General Machinery Corporation, Hamilton; 1,700BHP
As the USA progressed its war in the Pacific the need for a small, shallow-draughted ship able to supply the smaller ports became crucial and a new design, the C1-M-AV1, was added to the Commission's programme.

EGYPTOS
Consolidated Steel Corporation, Wilmington, California; 1945, 3,805g, 339 feet
Oil engine 2SCSA 6-cyl. by General Machinery Corporation, Hamilton; 1,700BHP
Perhaps the least attractive of all the cargo designs, the C1-M-AV1s were a popular choice with shipowners after the war particularly for their intermediate services, with even Cunard adding one to its fleet. Michael A. Embiricos acquired *Coastal Monitor* in 1947 and as *Krios* she joined his small collection of war-built tonnage. In 1961 she passed to the expanding Hellenic Line fleet of P. G. Callimanopoulos who ran her for a further 18 years as *Egyptos* but her lengthy career came to an end in 1980 when she was sold for breaking at Valencia after the main engine had failed. *[Roy Kittle collection]*

Solid Sinnet was launched just as the war was ending and the hull was later fitted out by Tampa Shipbuilding Co. as a C1-M-AV8 type for the French Government and named *Aulne*, managed by and subsequently sold to Compagnie de Navigation Paquet. As *Serene Med* she ran for the London-Greek owner D. Petropoulos's Med Line from 1965 until sold in 1972 to a Cypriot concern who kept her trading as *Athen* until she grounded off Port Harcourt in 1975. *[Roy Kittle]*

RILDA
Pacific Bridge Company, San Francisco; 1943, 1,825g, 259 feet.
T 3-cyl. by Pacific Bridge Company, San Francisco
A late addition to the programme were the small coastal steamers, the first group of which, designated N3-S-A1, were built at the request of the British and transferred under the Lend-Lease agreement. The design was based upon the traditional 'midships Baltic-type timber traders and in 1949 *Benjamin Sherburn*, like several of her sisters, was bought by one of the old established coasting companies who had earlier been involved in their management. She ran for Glen and Co. Ltd. as *Winga* until 1952 and then passed to a small Norwegian concern who acquired a further two ships of this type. As *Rilda* she was photographed on the Tyne in May 1962 but later ventured further afield and was broken up at Karachi in 1972 as the Kuwait owned *Raed*. *[Malcolm Donnelly]*

AMERICAN HUNTER (above)
Federal Shipbuilding and Dry Dock Company, Kearney; 1943, 8,433g, 459 feet
Two steam turbines double-reduction geared to a single shaft by General Electric Company, Lynn; 6,600 SHP
The C2 was the first of the Commission's cargo designs to enter service and with a total of 323 built over the next seven years it was the most numerous of all the 'C' types. The majority were of shelter-deck design and turbine driven. Both United States Lines and Lykes Brothers built up their post-war fleets largely with these ships with the former operating no fewer than 44 examples and *American Hunter* was one of 31 they had of the C2-S-B1 type. She had been built as *Cepheus* and ran initially on the United States Line's Pacific services as *Pioneer Sea* but in 1956 she was transferred to the East Coast to European routes and renamed. Twelve years later as *Brookville* she sustained considerable damage after running onto a coral reef and was abandoned. [*H.B. Cristiansen collection*]

TYSON LYKES (below)
North Carolina Shipbuilding Company, Wilmington, North Carolina; 1945, 8,191g, 459 feet
Two steam turbines double-reduction geared to a single shaft by General Electric Company, Lynn; 6,600 SHP
Lykes Brothers Steamship Co. Ltd. had a smaller but no less impressive number of C2s and *Tyson Lykes* was one of their 17 of the C2-S-AJ1 full scantling type. Like many of her sisters – and brothers – she was a frequent visitor to British ports particularly Liverpool and Manchester, bringing in cargoes from the US Gulf which included cotton for Lancashire's textile mills. To the young enthusiasts gathered at the end of New Brighton Pier on the Mersey, the particular preferences of the Lykes family members generated much juvenile humour. On this occasion *Tyson Lykes* had visited the Clyde and is seen on 2nd July 1965 outward bound passing Greenock. The distinctive 'bay window' front to the superstructure and pronounced bow rake are well displayed in this view. [*Malcolm Donnelly*]

DA GAMA (above)
Consolidated Steel Corporation, Wilmington, California;
1946, 6,103g, 460 feet
Two steam turbines double-reduction geared to a single
shaft by General Electric Company, Lynn; 6,600 SHP
No fewer than 113 of C2-S-B1 type were built and *Da
Gama* was one of the last ten ordered after the war.
Completed as *Ocean Rover* she soon moved to States
Marine Corporation as *Garden State*. Renamed *Margarett
Brown* after her sale in 1957, she became *Da Gama* in
1968 running for Crest Overseas Shipping Company, a
New York outfit of dubious standing. In September 1971,
on a voyage to Pakistan, she was arrested at Manila and
became involved in an international dispute. The port
authorities later took possession of the ship and she was
sold at auction for breaking in October 1972. Crest
Overseas other C2, *Ericson* - completed by the same
builders just a few weeks after *Da Gama* - was similarly
embroiled at Chittagong where she was finally broken up in
1978. Resplendent in her former States Marine colours,
Da Gama sails across San Francisco Bay in April 1969.
[Roy Kittle collection]

AMERICAN VICTORY (below)
*North Carolina Shipbuilding Corporation, Wilmington, North
Carolina; 1945, 8,228g, 459 feet*
*Two steam turbines double-reduction geared to a single
shaft by General Electric Company, Lynn; 6,600 SHP*
United States Lines had ten C2s built to their own
requirements which were designated C2-S-AJ5. The first
three of these were initially named in line the Maritime
Commission's theme of famous clipper ships and it was not
until 1947 that *Whistler* took their formulaic title as *Pioneer
Gem*. A move to the fleet of Farrell Lines' fleet in 1965 saw
a partial change of name to *Australian Gem* and with a
further change in ownership in 1969 came yet another new
prefixing as *Coral Gem*. In 1971 she became *American
Victory*, suggesting a return to United States Line's
ownership, although she now belonged to Victory Carriers
Inc., a US concern associated with Onassis. By 1974
when photographed at San Francisco she was among the
few surviving wartime built ships and when sold for
breaking in 1975 she was the last unmodified C2 still in
commercial service. *[Roy Kittle collection]*

SANTA ELIANA
Ingalls Shipbuilding Corporation, Pascagoula; 1944;
8,010g, 492 feet
Two steam turbines double-reduction geared to single shaft
by General Electric Company, Lynn; 9,350 SHP
The C3 ships exhibited many variations on the standard
designs with the basic hull configuration being adapted for
various naval duties, notably as escort carriers, tenders
and transports, with some of the latter being subsequently
converted into passenger ships. *Mendocino* was one of

many of the C3-S-A2 type built by Ingalls that were
completed as attack transports and she did not begin her
commercial life until 1947 as *P & T Seafarer*. Sold to
Moore-McCormack Line in 1957 and renamed *Mormacwind*
she ran for them until a further sale took her to Grace Line
in 1966 and is seen at Vancouver in 1970 as their *Santa
Eliana*. With her name shortened to *Eliana* she was broken
up in Taiwan in 1973. *[Steve Klassen, David Salisbury
collection]*

CITRUS PACKER
*Ingalls Shipbuilding Corporation,
Decatur;1945, 8,010g, 492 feet*
*Two steam turbines double-reduction
geared to single shaft by General Electric
Company, Lynn; 9,350 SHP*
The strangely-titled *Citrus Packer* was
acquired by Waterman Steamship
Corporation in 1969 and perpetuated the
name of an older C2 type sold by
Waterman some years previously.
Completed as *Sea Adder,* she was among
the first of the C3-S-A2 type ships to enter
directly into commercial service and her
cargo gear consequently differed
appreciably from that of the converted
Santa Eliana. From 1947 until her sale to
Waterman she had run as *American Mail*
for her eponymous owner's line. She was
broken up in 1975 *[Roy Kittle collection]*

GRAND UNITY
*Ingalls Shipbuilding Corporation,
Pascagoula; 1944, 7,901g, 492 feet*
*Two steam turbines double-
reduction geared to single shaft by General
Electric Company, Lynn; 9,350 SHP*
Matson Line acquired the *Sea
Falcon* in 1947 and ran her initially
as *Hawaiian Fisherman*. In 1962 she
was converted to a vehicle carrier
and with the posts carrying the fore-
and main masts removed, she re-
entered service as *Hawaiian
Motorist*. Sold in 1974 to the New
York-based Sea King Corporation –
whose funnel markings could easily
be mistaken for those of Brocklebank
– she was placed under the
Panamanian flag as *Grand Unity* and
scrapped up in 1978. *[Steve
Klassen, David Salisbury collection]*

EXBROOK

Bethlehem Sparrows Point Shipyard, Sparrows Point; 1946, 6,452g, 473 feet
Two steam turbines double-reduction geared to single shaft by Bethlehem Steel Corporation, Quincy; 8,800 SHP
In 1938 American Export Lines, in co-operation with the Maritime Commission, ordered four ships to its own design. Four more were ordered the following year which were given the designation C3-E and a subsequent order for fifteen very similar ships was designated C3-S-A3 type. All shared the same dated hull form with a counter stern as well displayed by *Exbrook* sailing from Durban. Renamed *Brook* after her sale to Great Neck Operating Corporation in 1975 she was scrapped the following year. *[Roy Kittle collection]*

TEXAS CLIPPER

Bethlehem Sparrows Point Shipyard, Sparrows Point; 1944, 9,644g, 473 feet
Two steam turbines double-reduction geared to single shaft by Bethlehem Steel Corporation, Quincy; 8,800 SHP
Nine of the C3-S-A3 ships were completed as naval transports but all were later acquired by American Export Lines and rebuilt. *Queens* was one of four chosen for extensive conversions to passenger-cargo liners which were to be replacements for the popular 'Four Aces' liners that had run before the war, and whose names they took. Withdrawn in 1959, *Excambion* went into lay-up but was re-commissioned in 1965 to become the training ship *Texas Clipper* for the Texas Aviation and Maritime Academy. Replaced by a newer ship many years ago, she still languishes awaiting disposal. *[Roy Kittle].*

GOLDEN BEAR

Bethlehem Sparrows Point Shipyard, Sparrows Point; 1940; 7,987g, 473 feet
Two steam turbines double-reduction geared to single shaft by Bethlehem Steel Corporation, Quincy; 8,800 SHP
Delorleans was one of six passenger-cargo ships of the C3-P and C Delta type originally ordered by the Mississippi Shipping Company, all of which were ultimately taken over by the US Navy. As USS *Crescent City* she served initially as an attack transport and later as a temporary hospital evacuation ship. Placed in reserve in 1948 she was re-activated 24 years later, re-fitted and began a new life as a school ship for the Californian Maritime Academy until laid up again in 1995. Four years later she was moved to Oakland to become an arts centre as the appropriately renamed *Artship* but unfortunately the scheme was abandoned. *[Roy Kittle collection]*

EMPIRE STATE IV

Ingalls Shipbuilding Corporation, Pascagoula; 1943, 12,069g, 473 feet
Two steam turbines double-reduction geared to single shaft by General Electric Company, Lynn; 9,350 SHP
Three ships of the C3-P P and C type were intended for United States Lines New York to London service but were taken over during construction and commissioned as army transports. Launched as *Biloxi* she served in various capacities as *Henry Gibbins* until 1959 when she was taken up by the New York State Maritime College as a training ship and renamed *Empire State IV*, seen here in June 1970 at Rotterdam. In 1974 she became *Bay State* and was scrapped in 1982. *[Roy Kittle]*

239

ROTTI
Sun Shipbuuilding and Dry Dock Company, Chester,
Pennsylvania; 1946, 8,358g, 492 feet
Two steam turbines double-reduction geared to single shaft
by General Electric Company, Erle; 8,500 SHP
Shortly after the end of the war the Netherlands
Government ordered ten ships of the C3-S-AJ5 type.

Built as the *Holland*, she was allocated to N.V. Stoomvaart
Maatschappij 'Nederland' and renamed *Rotti* while fitting
out. After what seems to have been an uneventful career
lasting 25 years she was delivered to Taiwan breakers at
the end of 1971, as were most of her consorts about his
time. *[G. Gould collection, World Ship Society Ltd.]*

SILVER DOVE
Ingalls Shipbuilding Corporation, Pascagoula;
1947, 7,667g, 492 feet
Two steam turbines double-reduction geared to
single shaft by General Electric Company,
Pittsburgh, 9,350 SHP
The C3-S-A5 type had been built to the special
requirements of Moore-McCormack Lines after
the war had ended and seven of these
operated for the company until 1970 when all
were sold. Four were bought by Oswego
Steamship Co. Inc. - a New York based
organisation linked to the Greek-managed
Allied Shipping International Corporation and
with complex connections to a host of other
concerns. At the beginning of 1973 only one of
these, the former *Mormacsaga*, remained in
service but on 2nd April shortly after having
cracks in her hull repaired at Guam, *Silver
Dove* foundered in calm seas off Johnston
Island in the Pacific. *[Roy Kittle collection]*

BENRINNES
Seattle-Tacoma Shipbuilding Corporation,
Tacoma; 1944, 8,008g, 492 feet
Two steam turbines double-reduction geared to
single shaft by Allis Chalmers Manufacturing
Company, Milwaukee; 8,500 SHP
The British Admiralty first proposed the use of
converted merchant ships to meet a desperate
need for escort carriers. This lead to over
seventy C3 hulls being so adapted of which 37
were transferred to the Royal Navy. Four of
the C3-S type were bought by British
companies after the war and *HMS Trouncer*
was one of two that went to Mollers for their
recently-acquired Lancashire Shipping
Company, becoming *Greystoke Castle*.
Chartered to Shaw Savill in 1954 she was
renamed *Gallic* and although purchased by Ben
Line three years later, she was not renamed
Benrinnes until 1959 on completion of the
charter. Towards the end of 1973 she was
demolished at Kaohsiung. *[Paul Boot]*

VALL MOON
*Sun Shipbuuilding and Dry Dock Company, Chester,
Pennsylvania; 1944, 11,562g, 520 feet*
*Two steam turbines double-reduction geared to single shaft
by General Electric Company, Erle; 9,900 SHP*
The C4 design was the largest of the Commission's cargo
ships and evolved from a design for the American-
Hawaiian Line. The military made a significant input to the
design and all but the first one of the initial order from this
yard were completed as troop transports or hospital ships
and designated C4-S-B2. *Marine Raven* was operated by
the War Shipping Administration until placed in reserve in
1948. After a lay up lasting 13 years she was converted to
a cargo ship and traded under a succession of names:
Sophie H., Vasso, Transpacific and finally *Vall Moon*. Boiler
damage brought about her demise in 1976 and she was
broken up at Karachi. *[Roy Kittle collection]*

KEYSTONE STATE (middle)
*Sun Shipbuuilding and Dry Dock Company, Chester,
Pennsylvania; 1945, 10,548g, 520 feet*
*Two steam turbines double-reduction geared to single
shaft by General Electric Company, Lynn; 9,900 SHP*
Marine Flier, one of the later C4-S-B5 type, was sold to
States Marine Corporation in 1951 but not renamed
Keystone State until 1955. Seen here at Southampton in
1966, she was sold for breaking in 1972. *[David
Bradbury]*

RIO COBRE (bottom)
*Gulf Shipbuilding Corporation, Chicksaw, Alabama; 1945,
6,845g, 455 feet*
*Two steam turbines double-reduction geared to single
shaft by De Laval Steam Turbine Company, Trenton;
12,000 SHP*
Elegant ships by any standards, the refrigerated
steamers ordered during the war by the United Fruit
Company contrasted starkly with the heavy purposeful
lines of the C4 ships and their predecessors. Originally
named *Junior* she became *Rio Cobre* when transferred
to Elders and Fyffes in 1969, and was scrapped in 1975.
[G. Gould collection, World Ship Society Ltd.]

241

TOLTEC (top)
Newport News Shipbuilding and Dry Dock Company, Newport News; 1947, 6,573g, 455 feet
Two steam turbines double-reduction geared to single shaft by De Laval Steam Turbine Company, Trenton; 12,000 SHP
Nine of the R2-ST-AU1 type refrigerated ships were built for United Fruit and all had long successful careers, initially under the American flag but later transferred to the British and Dutch subsidiaries. Formerly *Parismina* she became *Toltec* in 1970 and was operated by Caraibische Scheepsvaart Maatschappij until withdrawn in 1976. A notable feature of these ships was the cruiser stern with its very prominent propeller guards. [Roy Kittle]

CIBAO (middle)
Bethlehem Sparrows Point Shipyard, Sparrows Point; 1947, 5,026g, 386 feet
Two steam turbines double reduction geared to single shaft by De Laval Steam Turbine Company, Trenton, 6,050 SHP
The smaller R1-S-DH1 ships which followed were no less graceful with the pronounced counter sterns, still beloved of the Bethlehem company, giving them a particularly yacht-like appearance. *Cibao* moved to the Van Nievelt, Goudriaan managed Dutch fleet in 1970 as *Cholutuca* and was scrapped at Bruges in 1975.
[G. Gould collection, World Ship Society Ltd.]

COPAN (bottom)
Bethlehem Sparrows Point Shipyard, Sparrows Point; 1947, 5,127g, 386 feet
Two steam turbines double-reduction geared to single shaft by De Laval Steam Turbine Company, Trenton; 6,050 SHP
The former *Quisqueya*, *Copan* had taken the Dutch flag barely a year before this photograph was taken in September 1970. Despite the rusting hull and addition of the Chiquita 'banana label' logo she still makes a fine sight and remained in service for another five years. [G. Gould collection, World Ship Society Ltd.]

THE DRESDEN WHITE FLEET INTO THE 21ST CENTURY
F.W. Hawks

Sächsischen Dampfschiffarts Gesellschaft (the Saxony Steamship Company) was founded in 1836, from a suggestion by two Dresden businessmen, Benjamin Schwenke and Friedrich Lange, to operate steamship services on the River Elbe, based at Dresden. Some 167 years later it is still operating, although there have been alterations to the name and, from 1928, the company has also been known as the Dresden White Fleet from the hull colour of its vessels.

The first vessel in the fleet was the locally-built paddle steamer *Königin Maria* (36 metres long, carrying 350 passengers), which made its maiden voyage from Dresden down river to Meissen on 30th July 1837. Two more vessels, *Prinz Albert* and *Dresden*, appeared the following year and, during the subsequent 165 years the company went on to acquire a further 66 paddle steamers, four large diesel-electric paddle vessels, and eight motor vessels. For various reasons, a considerable amount of renaming of the vessels has taken place over the years, so that they have carried no less than 125 names between them, although there has been quite a lot of duplication of names. The fleet reached its maximum size in 1899/1900 when 38 vessels were listed in company ownership.

Nine of the paddle steamers, including seven of the present fleet, have survived for more than a century, the most venerable being the current *Stadt Wehlen* of 1879, which has so far achieved 124 years, albeit with a degree of rebuilding and engine/boiler replacement.

In 1841 the paddle steamer *Bohemia* was launched in Prague by the English shipbuilder Joseph Rushton, who ran the vessel on a competing service between Tetschen and Dresden, following with *Germania* in 1845. A Captain Naumann from Dresden entered the fray in 1848 with *Constitution*, but all three of the competing vessels were acquired in 1851.

In 1877, in recognition of the fact that services were operating across the border into Bohemia, the company was renamed Sächsisch-Böhmischen Dampfschiffahrts Gesellschaft (SBDG) (Saxony Bohemia Steamship Co.) which title was to be retained until 1923. A further rationalisation of the upper Elbe services in the latter year resulted in the amalgamation of SBDG with the Neuen Deutsch-Böhmische-Elbschiffahrts-Gesellschaft to form Sächsisch-Böhminsche Dampfschiffahrt Aktiengesellschaft (SBDA) which lasted until after the Second World War.

In 1945 six vessels were transferred to Czechoslovak ownership and, under the German Democratic Republic (East Germany) nationalisation, in 1948 ownership of the remainder of the fleet was transferred to VEB Elbeschiffahrt Sächsen.

Emblem on the paddle box of *Pirna*.

Centralisation went further in 1950, when the fleet became part of Deutsche Schiffahrts-und Umschlagsbetriebszentrale (DSU) (German Shipping and Central Management Department), with headquarters in Potsdam. Another change came six years later, with a degree of independence under the title VEB Fahrgastschiff Dresden Weisse Flotte. After German reunification, in 1992 the company reverted almost to its original 1836 title, although, as part of the Conti group the full title is Sächsische Dampfschiffahrts GmbH & Co. Conti Elbschiffahrts KG.

Four diesel-electric paddle vessels were brought into the fleet in the early 1960s with good communist names *Karl Marx*, *Friedrich Engels*, *Wilhelm Pieck*, and *Ernst Thälmann*. After reunification they were all renamed in 1991, but the first two were disposed of in 1992 to become youth hostels elsewhere in Germany. The other two were renamed *August Der Starke* and *Gräfin Cosel*, and survived until being broken up in 1998, although the names were reallocated to two large motor vessels in 1994. These were constructed to have a superficial resemblance to paddlers, with the passenger entrance being through the centre of the 'paddle box'.

The steamers all had their accommodation modernised in the early 1990s, and, with the exception of *Diesbar*, which remains coal-fired, were converted to oil-fired boilers.

The company entered the 21st century with nine active paddle steamers: *Stadt Wehlen* (launched as *Dresden* in 1879), *Diesbar* (1884, ex-*Pillnitz*), *Meissen* (1885, ex-*König Albert*), *Pillnitz* (1886, ex-*Königin Carola*), *Krippen* (1892, ex-*Tetschen*), *Kurort Rathen* (1896, ex-*Bastei*), *Pirna* (1898, ex-*König Albert*), *Dresden* (1926) and *Leipzig* (1929); two motor vessels *August Der Starke* (1994) and *Gräfin Cosel* (1994); two laid-up paddle steamers: *Schmilka* (1897, ex-*Hohenzollern*) and *Junger Pionier* (1898, ex-*Karlsbad*); together with a number of small motor launches. The laid-up vessels had been taken out of service in 1984 and 1987 respectively, and were scrapped in 2002.

In 2003, *Krippen* operated down-river services between Dresden and Meissen, while the other vessels operated non-landing excursions and up-river services through the picturesque 'Saxon Switzerland' to various riverside townships. *Pirna* continued up-river from Bad Schandau to Decin (formerly Tetschen) in the Czech Republic. As this route crossed an international border, the steamer was entitled to carry a duty-free shop, at least until the Czech Republic joined the European Community!

[Note: this article was based on the situation in 2003]

Stadt Wehlen, launched as *Dresden* in 1879 and now the oldest in the fleet, under way on the River Elbe on 27th July 1995. *[All photographs by the Author]*

Above: The only coal fired vessel remaining in the fleet is the *Diesbar* of 1884, formerly the *Pillnitz and* seen here moored at Dresden on 6th July 2003.

Left: The paddle steamer *Meissen*, completed in 1885 as the *König Albert*, approaching Kurort Rathen on 8th July 2003.

Pillnitz, completed in 1886 as *Königin Carola*, leaving Kurort Rathen for Dresden in July 2003.

Above: Built as *Bastei* in 1896, *Kurort Rathen* berthed at Pirna on 27th July 1995.

Left: Pirna (1898, ex-*König Albert*) arriving at Koenigstein 27th July 1995.

Left: *Dresden*, completed in 1926, on the River Elbe on 27th July 1995.

Middle: *Leipzig,* which was completed in 1929, at Pirna on 27th July 1995.

Gräfin Cosel, one of the two motor vessels completed in 1994, taking passengers on board at Dresden on 8th July 2003. *Gräfin Cosel* and her sister ship *August Der Starke* replaced two diesel-electric paddle ships of the same names which had been scrapped in 1998.

SD14
SOME RECENT DEVELOPMENTS

Tania (Austin and Pickersgill, Southwick yard No. 1377). With sightings of SD14s becoming fewer Silvio Smera was particularly fortunate to capture *Tania* (9,213/1978) arriving in Santos on 10th Septmber 2005. Carrying the Georgian flag she came to load a cargo of 14,000 tons of sugar, in bags, for Tema, Ghana. Originally named *Empros* she was effectively the first of the 'Fourth Series' design to be built, although her main engine was of the earlier (5RND68) Sulzer type. Launched in November 1977 a dispute with the owning principal, George Dracopoulos, lead to her being initially unnamed and it was not until the following July that she finally entered service for Empros Lines. Like all of the ships operated by this company she was always well maintained and the present owners of this 27 year old ship seem to be upholding the tradition.

Presidente Ramon S. Castillo (AFNE, yard No. 51). Until a few weeks ago the survival of this Argentinean built and owned ship had been in doubt. She had become one of the dozen or so SD14s whose movements had ceased to be recorded in recent years and was last reported to be laid up at Ibicuy, a small port on a tributary of the Parana River, since June 1996. Surprisingly as this photograph shows she is still there, probably abandoned and certain never to trade again. *[Charlie Ney]*

The *Safmarine Namibe* (CCN yard number 159) at Durban, showing the new container crane on her port side. [*Trevor Jones*]

Above: The recently renamed *Ryu Gyong* (CCN yard number 158) photographed at Singapore, 25th June 2005. [*Nigel Jones*]

Right: Xin He Er Hao, Bartram's yard number 440, without cargo gear. [*Courtesy David Hazell*]

SD14 ADDITIONS AND UPDATES

Published last autumn by Ships in Focus, 'SD14 – The Full Story' by John Lingwood has been very well received ('excellent and comprehensive' said the journal 'The Naval Architect'). Author and publishers are particularly gratified that virtually no errors have been detected in the text, despite the interest shown in these ships by enthusiasts and the complexity of some of the ships' histories. The relatively few changes to surviving ships reported since publication, plus a few corrections to dates and credits of photographs, are noted below. Much of this comes from Nigel Jones and from David Hazell of The Shipping Information Service, and updates the 'Survivors' list on page 40 in 'Record' 29.

Updates and corrections

Page 45: the *Sinfa* was trading when photographed in 1998, not laid up as was surmised in the caption.

Page 63: the name on the stern of the ship appears to be *Jang Dae San*.

Page 68: photo credit for *Catharina Oldendorff* should be to David Salisbury.

Page 71 and 75: photo credits for *Ajana* and *African Express* should be to Don Brown.

Page 78: it was incorrect to claim that the *Lundoge* had been continuously laid up at Luanda with mechanical problems since being damaged by a mine in 1984. Trevor Jones recorded her at Durban in 1993, and although she was in 'utterly decrepit condition', she worked cargo for several days and then sailed. Trevor's researches in 'Lloyd's Shipping Index' indicate that she was at least partly active between November 1990 and October 1995, when she was again laid up in Luanda Bay with generator problems, which have seemingly kept her inactive since.

Page 79: the *Song Duong* was photographed on 20th June 1980 not in March 1983.

Page 84: the *Fortunate Star* was photographed on 26th June 1998 not 1993.

Pages 90/1: following repairs, it is believed the *Spring's* only movement was to Batam Island, Indonesia where she has remained idle. Her present owners and flag have not been established.

Page 93: *Shun Yuan 6* is now trading as *New Legend Star* under the Hong Kong flag.

Page 103: *Odelis* (the last Sunderland-built SD14) was sold to Poditi Holdings S.A., Greece and renamed *Theofilos* under the Panama flag early in 2005, but has since been reported sold to Indian breakers.

Page 119: the *Mandarin Ocean* was photographed on 25th June 1997 not 1967.

Page 131: Bartram's yard number 440 was photographed in Chinese waters during 2005 with the name *Xin He Er Hao*. Her cargo-gear has been removed.

Page 155: the photograph of *Erodios* was supplied by Russell Priest, but was actually taken by Roger Hurcombe in Singapore's Eastern Anchorage on 23rd January 2001.

Page 165: photo credit for *Scapwind* should be to Bernard Morton.

Page 177: the *Kum Gang* may still be with us: she was reported sailing from Singapore in January 2004, and should be added to the survivors' list.

Page 214: in contrast, it looks like the *Oriental Peace* may have to be deleted from the survivors' list. She was due to be renamed *Veesham Trader III*, and vessels with a similar name/number are usually destined for Indian shipbreaking yards.

Page 215: in 2005 the *Long Xiang* was sold to Sinhung Shipping Co., North Korea as *Ryu Gyong*.

Page 216: the *Jordan II* has been sold to Fude Maritime Ltd., based in China, and renamed *Fude* under the flag of St. Vincent and the Grenadines.

Page 222: the report that the North Korean SD14 *Eun Bong* had become a casualty was erroneous – she was confused with another vessel. *Eun Bong* was still trading when sighted in Japan during April 2005.

Page 225: Unexpectedly, *Presidente Ramon S. Castillo* is still afloat; she was photographed laid up on the River Parana at Ibicuy, Argentina in April 2005.

Page 227: the Cuban *Lotus Islands* was sold to Lekfield Shipping Inc., Panama and renamed *Weng* in 2004.

Page 241: the *Oriental Honour* was sold in 2001 to the Government of the People's Republic of North Korea and renamed *Green*.

SAFWAF SD14s

Just when the steady movement of SD14s towards the Far Eastern scrap yards seemed to be suggesting that the fascinating career of this ageing Liberty ship replacement was drawing to a close, four vessels, built in Brazil by Companhia Comercio e Navegacao (CCN), under licence from designers Austin and Pickersgill of Sunderland, have gained a new lease of life operating on charter to Safmarine, maintaining that company's SAFWAF (South Africa/West Africa) service, which links ports on both coasts of the continent via the Cape. Three of the vessels, now sailing as *Safmarine Evagelia*, *Safmarine Meroula* and *Safmarine Congo* are actually owned by companies controlled by Athens-based Pitiousa Shipping S.A., whilst the fourth was acquired in September 2004 from Chinese principals, especially for this charter, by Aurelia Reederei Eugen Friederich G.m.b.H. Schiffahrtsges. & Co. K.G., of Bremen.

The basic cargo gear specification of the SD14 consisted of derrick booms at each hatch, usually operated by winches in a union purchase configuration, and occasionally enhanced by the fitting of a heavy lift derrick varying in capacity from 20 tonnes to 120 tonnes swl. In later vessels, and particularly in those built in Sunderland, this time-honoured arrangement was often replaced by the more sophisticated 'swinging derrick' system in which a single, centreline-mounted boom was operated exactly as with a deck crane by one man using a joy-stick controller. With capacities of at least 25 tonnes swl, these high-speed derricks could handle containers and packaged cargoes effectively and proved very popular.

Many CCN-built vessels, however, were fitted with various combinations of self-contained, totally enclosed deck cranes, complementing a reduced outfit of conventional derricks, whilst others, like the four sisters now operating on the SAFWAF service, were delivered only with two 'twin' cranes positioned between numbers 1 and 2, and 3 and 4 hatchways, respectively, and a pair of 10 tonne derricks behind the deckhouse serving number 5 hatch. Each crane unit in this configuration comprised a platform, mounted on a centreline pedestal revolving through 360°. On this platform two deck cranes were positioned, revolving individually and, depending on the positioning of the central platform, capable of working cargo either singly, serving adjacent holds, or linked with its partner to provide twice the lift at either hatch.

For the SAFWAF service the four vessels, built as *Bianca*, *Ana Luisa*, *Alessandra* and *Renata* respectively, have had their container carrying facility enhanced by the fitting of deck supports and more recently by an interesting retrofit involving the addition of a port-side mounted crane, positioned between numbers 2 and 3 hatches, and of the type more usually seen on new building multi-purpose vessels, in fact, Ships in Focus understands that the first three vessels named were modified in Durban using redundant cranes removed earlier from ships of this type, whilst *Safmarine Namibe* (see page 248) was similarly converted in China.
JOHN LINGWOOD, 32 Nursery Lane, Sunderland

Beached, but not for breaking
Congratulations to all concerned in the production of the SD 14 book.

The photograph of *Uniselva* on page 184 'beached, apparently for breaking' was taken at Manila in October 1993, the day after Typhoon Flo had passed over the city. Although typhoons are a regular occurrence in the Philippines at that time of the year, Manila's location on the western side of the island of Luzon typically affords the city some protection from the full force of the storms as the mountains in the centre of the island seem to deflect the storm northwards. On this occasion, however, the typhoon passed directly over Manila. Faced with this unexpected turn of events, *Uniselva* was one of several vessels which delayed their departure from the Manila anchorage until after the storm had passed. However, one or two ships got underway, their crews apparently unaware that Flo had a sting in her tail.

While still in the anchorage, *Uniselva* lost power and collided with at least one other vessel and a couple of barges before grounding in the north east corner of Manila Bay, close to the perimeter wall of the US Embassy, and even closer to the stem of the small tanker *Camiguin* which had beached broadside to the sea wall.

Her master's interview with Manila's Lloyd's Agent, Freddy Clemo OBE, included the following, possibly apocryphal, exchange: Master 'Am I aground, technically speaking?' Agent 'Another few yards and you would be blocking traffic on Roxas Boulevard. Sir, you may consider yourself aground!'

She was refloated and sailed for Singapore, arriving on 24th October. She was in the western anchorage off Pulau Bukom four weeks later, still with the dent in her forepeak.
SIMON OLSEN, The Old Stables, 28 Mill Road, Buckden, Cambridgeshire PE19 5SS

Some Disadvantages
Having sailed on an SD14 (*Belloc*) I sometimes thought SD stood for 'steel dungeon' because they were great to work on but not to sleeep on, especially when working cargo in the tropics with number 4 hatch covers folding up against the bridge front. This was a carryover from the original design when they did not have mast houses and had their winches on top of main deck cabins. As third engineer I was classified as a junior officer and so was not allowed two windows and so there was no forward facing window on the port side corner of the bridge front, although this was not a great loss when carrying containers. My cabin felt like it included a four-foot day bed and a six-foot desk.

Belloc was fitted with one-man-operated Velle derricks but when stores were taken on the aft derrick had to be used, needing the best part of the crew to rig it for a five minute job, and it could not be used for main engine parts. I often wondered why she was the only one of the sisters not to have her forecastle bulwarks painted white.

Having seen Tony Lofthouse's cut-away drawing over the years I wonder if your readers can spot the mistake? Compare the aft hatch covers with those on number 3 hatch: they are the wrong way round.
A.D.FROST, 32 Oakfield Close, Sunderland, SR3 3RT

Available in English and German
'SD14: the full story' is published in both English and German language versions. It offers a fresh, first-hand account of conception and planning from a member of the design team. Career details are included of 228 ships: every SD14, the Prinasa-121s, the SD15 and SD18s. Every one is illustrated, usually at several stages of its career, almost entirely in colour. 'SD14: the full story' is available from J. & M. Clarkson, 18 Franklands, Longton, Preston,PR4 5PD, UK at £29.50 plus £3.50 postage.

SOURCES AND ACKNOWLEDGEMENTS

We thank all who gave permission for their photographs to be used, and for help in finding photographs we are particularly grateful to Tony Smith, Jim McFaul and David Whiteside of the World Ship Photo Library; to Ian Farquhar, F.W. Hawks, Peter Newall, Ivor Rooke, William Schell, George Scott; and to David Hodge and Bob Todd of the National Maritime Museum, and other museums and institutions listed.

Research sources have included the *Registers* of William Schell and Tony Starke, *Lloyd's Register*, *Lloyd's Confidential Index*, *Lloyd's War Losses*, *Mercantile Navy Lists*, *Marine News* and *Shipbuilding and Shipping Record*. Use of the facilities of the World Ship Society's Central Record, the Guildhall Library, the Public Record Office and Lloyd's Register of Shipping are gratefully acknowledged, and Dr Malcolm Cooper is thanked for checking Second World War losses. Particular thanks also to Heather Fenton for editorial and indexing work, and Marion Clarkson for accountancy services.

The white fleet of Thor Dahl
Many thanks to: Dag Bakka for sharing his extensive knowledge of Norwegian shipping, in particular Thor Dahl; Bill Schell for ensuring the fleet list was as accurate as possible and in Cape Town to: Andrew Ingpen, Brian Ingpen, Robert Pabst and Ian Shiffman for providing such excellent photographs.

SELIM'S SD14 DEMOLITIONS

Top and middle: The breakers at work on *Litsa* (CCN yard number 104) at Aliaga. She arrived for breaking up on 8th August 2001. *[Selim San]*

Bottom: *Dawn* (Bartram yard number 455) on 27th May 2002, three days after arrival at Aliaga. *[Selim San]*

CONSTRUCTIONAL PHOTOGRAPHS OF SD14S
John Lingwood

It was unfortunate that when 'SD14 – The Full Story' was being prepared a year ago, no photographs of vessels under construction could be found; now, a year later, thanks to the efforts of Tyne and Wear Archives, a small collection has been located and examples are included here. In all 126 SD14s were completed in Sunderland, and it is tempting to always associate these with the Southwick shipyard of designer Austin & Pickersgill, arguably the most modern yard in Europe at the time. However, 54 of these vessels were built in an unbroken sequence over 10 years at the tiny South Dock shipyard of Bartram and Sons (later taken over by A & P) which launched directly into the North Sea, had few modern facilities and was exposed to often dreadful weather conditions. Despite these handicaps the yard's annual output closely matched that of the parent yard. The photographs shown are of two vessels, *Industria* (yard number 454) and *Dunelmia* (2) (460) built in the South Dock yard in 1976 and 1977.

Above and right: With the first double bottom units in place about midships, transverse bulkheads and midship side-shell panels could next be erected using the mono-tower travelling cranes. (At Southwick much larger units could be handled).

Keel blocks support more double bottom units as erection moves forward. The port side standing launchway can also be seen, and some 'tween deck pontoon hatch covers lie to one side in a storage area awaiting fitting when the ship nears completion.

Erection on the berth moved both forward and aft from the starting point simultaneously, although much of the structure would only be 'tack-welded' together and supported by timber shores at this stage.

As the last stern units were positioned, the stern frame could be accurately put in place to ensure alignment with the main engine and shafting. Note that in this illustration, work has commenced adding sections of the aft deck, whilst the keel blocks and standing launch ways are also in evidence. A hazard of the South Dock yard was that this area of the building berths would often be flooded at high tide, or silted up with sand after stormy North Sea weather.

On the berth, erection of the ship has almost reached the bow, and the lower section shown in the earlier photograph, and the upper bow unit depicted here which includes the soft nose stem, internal stringers and a portion of deck, will soon be placed in position.

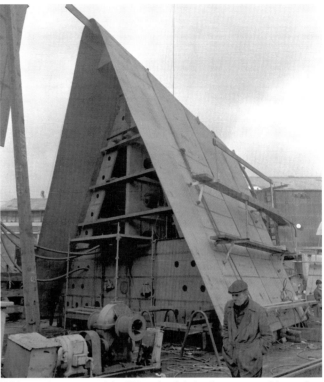

Without the covered facilities for fabrication, assembly and erection available at Southwick, this work had to be carried out in the open adjacent to the building berths. Here a lower fore end unit is being assembled.

A general view of internal fore end structure, looking into the forward hold. An upper deck hatch coaming forms a frame to the top of the picture, with parts of the second deck coaming and 'tween deck centreline bulkhead in the centre. At the bottom, the side shell with the large tankside brackets which connect it to the double bottom, can be seen curving in towards the bow. *[All photographs courtesy of Tyne & Wear Archives Service]*

WHAT DAY WAS THIS?
Graeme Sommer

This is an aerial view of Leith Docks, but in what year, on what day, and at what time was it taken? What clues are there which can tell us this? Fortunately certain Leith Dock Commission documents concerning the movement of vessels within Leith still exist, and using them in-conjunction with copies of 'Lloyd's Lists' of the time can give us a fair estimation of when the photograph was taken. What are the clues?

The plane that took this picture was flying north to south just to the west of the port and was probably over the fishing harbour of Newhaven. Working from the top left the eastern half of the Imperial Dock is visible. The Water of Leith with its riverside tidal berths runs across from left to right (running roughly north to south) of the picture, with the Victoria Dock and the East Old Dock (with just the tip of the West Old Dock visible in the right corner) below it. Above the line of the Water of Leith are Number 1 and 2 Dry Docks, the Albert Dock, and beyond the Edinburgh Dock with the grain elevator at the far end.

Many of the ships in dock can be positively identified. Starting at the Imperial Dock, we have the Newcastle-registered *Cairnmona* (4,666/1918) and *Cairndhu* (5,250/1919) owned by the Cairn Line of Steamers Ltd. lying laid-up, the former we know was there from 4th June 1930 until 6th October 1931, and the latter from 15th December 1929 until 7th September 1931. On the south quay of the Imperial Dock are moored three of the port's tugs. The two-funnelled screw tug is the *Herwit* (256/1904), ahead is the paddle tug *Flying Fish* (169/1882), and ahead of her the screw tug *R. Nicholson* (200/1891).

Looking at the vessels berthed in the tidal Water of Leith, on the extreme left we have the General Steam Navigation Company's berth at which are the steamers *Woodlark* (1,801/1928) and astern of her *Peregrine* (938/1921). Both sailed between London and Leith, with *Woodlark* (on the loading berth) taking the Saturday sailing, and the *Peregrine* (at the discharge berth) having just arrived from London on a Saturday morning. Astern of the General Steam Navigation steamers in the Albert Dock Basin lies the Glasgow owned *Navarino* (5,103/1907) laid-up at Leith for about three years between 1930 and 1933, with the tug *Oxcar* (252/1919) berthed alongside. A little further upstream on the opposite bank, lying at Hermitage Wharf at right angles to each other, are the London and Edinburgh Shipping Company steamers *Royal Fusilier* (2,187/1924) in the loading berth, and astern of her in the discharging berth is *Royal Scot* (1,444/1930). *Royal Scot* was a new vessel and only came into service on 5th April 1930. *Royal Fusilier* always sailed (depending on the tide) on a Saturday afternoon after 2.00 pm, whilst *Royal Scot* arrived from London early on a Saturday morning and moved into the loading berth after the Saturday departure. The berthing positions of all four of these vessels tells us that the photograph was taken on a Saturday afternoon. The fact is that there is so little activity in the docks further confirms the time was a weekend.

Moving yet further upstream we can see in the Victoria Dock two large steamers owned by the Leith, Hull and Hamburg Steam Packet Company. The steamer at the top of the quay could be either the three-masted *Breslau* (1,366/1882) or sister ship *Coblenz* (1,338/1883), sailing on alternate Wednesdays to Hamburg. Astern is one of

Woodlark of 1928 had a long career with General Steam, and when sold in 1954 steamed on, first as *Halcyon Med* in the Mediterranean and after 1956 as *Asha* for Bombay owners. After almost 40 years' work, she was broken up in India in 1967. *[Graeme Sommer collection]*

Cairnmona, laid up at Leith when the aerial photograph was taken, returned to service but was an early war loss, torpedoed and sunk by the German submarine U 13 off Rattray Head on 30th October 1939 when on a voyage with Canadian wheat for the Tyne and Leith. *[B. & A. Feilden/J. & M. Clarkson]*

another pair of steamers that sailed on alternative weeks to Bremen, *Oder* (965/1909) or *Corsica* (1,100/1895). As records show that *Oder* was in Number 2 Dry Dock, the vessel must be *Corsica*.

In the Water of Leith above the swing bridge lies one of the Leith, Hull and Hamburg Steam Packet Company's steamers that operate the Newcastle and Hull sailings, the sister ships *Britannia* (623/1918) or *Edina* (624/1918). The former took the Saturday sailing, the latter the Wednesday, so the vessel must be *Britannia*. Just across from that berth in the dry dock owned by Menzies and Co., ship repairers, lies the Northern Light Commissioners' tender *Pole Star* (459/1892) which had arrived from her base at Stromness, Orkney, for her annual survey on 1st July 1930.

In the north west corner of the East Old Dock are a group of laid-up vessels. On the inside is the Leith, Hull and Hamburg Steam Packet Company's *Hague* (974/1919) – her sister ship *Haarlem* was in service and arrived at Leith on 18th August. Outside *Hague* is the same company's spare steamer *Stettin* (706/1864). The identity of the sailing vessel is unknown but the tug outside her is the local *Earl of Powis* (116/1882). Astern of this group in her normal berth when not at sea is the Fishery Protection Cruiser *Norna* (457/1909).

In the centre of Albert Dock are moored the Leith, Hull and Hamburg Steam Packet Company's sister ships *Helder* (999/1920) and *Helmond* (983/1921). *Helder* (probably the vessel on the left with the cleaner bridge paintwork) was laid-up from 25th January 1930 until 22nd August 1930 and *Helmond* from 31st January 1930 until 4th September 1931, which confirms that the picture could not have been taken later than 22nd August 1930. Also in that dock is the North of Scotland, Orkney and Shetland Steam Navigation Company's *St Catherine* (1,065/1893) in her usual weekend berth between trips to the Northern Isles.

Above: *Helder* was also acquired from Halcyon Lijn, for whom she had been built as *Stad Schiedam*. She too was sold in 1945, first becoming Comben Longstaff's *Sussexbrook* and quickly Limerick Steamship's *Kilfenora*. Passing to Bombay owners in 1954, she was broken up in 1960. [Graeme Somner collection]
Below: *St Catherine* was built for Laird Line as *Olive*, becoming *Lairdsbank* when Laird's and Burn's interests were amalgamated under Coast Lines' ownership. She was transferred to the North of Scotland company and renamed in 1930, and was broken up at Rosyth in 1937. [Graeme Somner collection]

Haarlem's name was not the only link with Holland, she had been built at Kampen as *Stad Kampen* for Halcyon Lijn. Acquired by Leith, Hull and Hamburg in 1922, she survived the war to be sold in 1945, being renamed *Andromachi*, *Isle of Ithaca* and *Katy* in the nine years she had left until broken up. [Graeme Somner collection]

Turning now to the east side of the Water of Leith, dry docks Number 1 and Number 2 are both occupied. Number 1 (the left hand one) is taken up by Christian Salvesen's whale supply ship *Ravenstone* (3,049/1905) in port between 19th July and 19th September 1930. The vessel in Number 2 Dry Dock is the Leith, Hull and Hamburg Steam Packer Company's *Oder* (965/1909) which had arrived from Bremen on 31st July. She next sailed on 25th August after her annual survey.

pictures. He determined that the time was about 4.00 pm (from the clock face on the North British Hotel in Princes Street) and that both cricket and football matches were being played at the time. These games are hardly likely to be played in July but certainly would have been in August. He established that the cricket season in 1930 finished in mid/late August, and that football league season started on 9th August. He therefore suggested the flight was made on a Saturday in August 1930.

Can we assume that Saturday 2nd August or 16th August 1930 was the date? The fact that certain vessels were in port restricts the date – *Brandon* was in port from 8th July until 4th November, *Scottish Prince* arrived on 20th June and sailed on 20th August, whilst *Helder* was laid-up on 25th January 1930 until brought into service again on 22nd August. On those dates *Breslau* was berthed in Victoria Dock, as was *Corsica*. *Pentland Firth* had arrived from the north on both Fridays but moved berth on 5th August for repairs, although was available for the sailing a fortnight later.

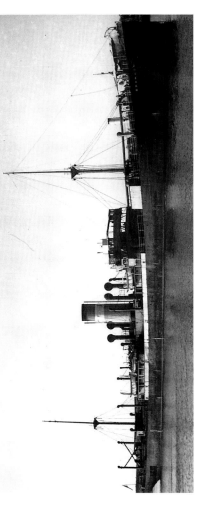

Salvesen's *Brandon* had been built in Sunderland as *Holbrook* for London owners, quickly being sold to Canadian Pacific Railway who in 1923 renamed her first as *Bredon* then within a few months *Brandon*. Salvesen bought her in 1928, and lost her on 8th December 1939 when she was torpedoed by U 48 150 miles west of Land's End whilst sailing in ballast to North America. [Graeme Somner collection]

The flood tide appears to be well up with the dock gates normally being opened some two-to-three hours prior to high water. On the 2nd that would be about 6.30 pm and 5.0 pm on the 16th. The state of the tide in the picture makes the 16th the more probable date. The position of all the vessels identified would be exactly the same on both dates.

On balance, taking the state of the tide into account, the photograph was taken on a calm, clear summer afternoon at about 4.00 pm on Saturday 16th August 1930. The gates to the enclosed docks would be opening in about an hour or so, and the usual crowd to see passengers off to London on *Royal Fusilier* have yet to assemble to wave their friends off on what was probably a 7.00 pm sailing.

I am indebted to Captain John Landels for his help in providing me with dates of arrival and departure of certain ships.

Third of Leith, Hull and Hamburg's ships, *Minorca* was photographed arriving at Grangemouth with timber from the Baltic on 22nd February 1936. She was built at Goole for Norwegian owners as *Lysland*, but in 1922 was bought by a Liverpool owner who renamed her *Aughton*. When she went out of business in 1925, she passed to the Leith, Hull and Hamburg Steam Packet Co. Ltd. and was renamed. *Minorca* was sunk by a German motor torpedo boat off Cromer on 26th February 1941. [Graeme Somner collection]

Ships in the far distant Edinburgh Dock are rather more difficult to identify. The two tied to the quay bow on are likely to be *Minorca* (1,123/1921) and *Inverawe* (2,196/1914), both owned by Leith, Hull and Hamburg Steam Packet Company. It is known that the sister ship of *Minorca*, named *Majorca*, called at Leith on 31st July but sailed the next day. The large ship moored at the top of the north branch of the dock is *Scottish Prince* (2,897/1910) owned by Prince Lines Ltd. of Newcastle-upon-Tyne, in port from 20th June to 20th August. Tied-up in the south branch of the dock is another of Christian Salvesen's steamers, *Brandon* (6,665/1917), in port from 8th July 1930 until 4th November 1930 for annual repairs. In the south west corner of that dock there is the small coaster *Pentland Firth* (423/1915) employed sailing between Leith and Moray Firth ports. She had arrived back from Inverness on 1st August 1930, having unfortunately struck the ground while entering Lossiemouth the day before. She was moved into the East Old Dock for repair on 5th August, but sailed again on 18th August.

What was the time of day? By the angle of the shadows from the warehouses and other buildings it was a late summer afternoon, and the time is confirmed by the fact that the Saturday London steamers have not yet sailed. Why had they not sailed – because the tide was late in the day. The lock gates to the enclosed docks were normal opened about two-to-three hours before high water, but they are closed in the photograph. By the drift of the flow from the exhaust outlet of *Peregrine* the tide is on the flood. The only Saturdays in August 1930 that had late evening tides were 2nd August (9.39 pm) and 16th August (7.56 pm).

Which date was it? As it happens this photograph was taken with a whole batch of others covering Edinburgh, and published recently under the title of 'Old Edinburgh – Views from Above'. John Jones the author also tried to establish the date of these

FROM THE BOSUN'S LOCKER
John Clarkson

When 'From the Bosun's Locker' first appeared in 'Record' 29 it was stated we would try to carry items of as wide a variety as possible. To date we have mainly dealt with photographs and, unfortunately, obituaries. In this issue I would like to expand the cover by writing about a little book I recently came across.

Dirty Little Collier was written by John Batten and published by Hutchinson. There is no year given but looking at the paper I would guess at the late 1940s. There are many books to be had on what it was like on deep-sea ships during the Second World War, both the lucky ones which lasted the war out and on the others which did not, but there is little about life on coasters.

John Batten, radio officer for nine months, describes what it was like on the *Hampden Z. Coney*, an American-built ship, as he says, with a queer cowl on her funnel and the red ensign of the British Merchant Navy flying from her stern. Searching registers will not provide any details of the ship. In the dedication to Captain James F Clark, of South Shields and to John's shipmates it transpires that the real name of the ship was *Laban Howes.*

The first chapter book tells about the East Coast coal trade on which she served, the conditions onboard, even down to the meals on which they survived. Later chapters tell of individual voyages, problems encountered (wanting to keep a diary was one), and the good times had despite the war. John tells of the struggles with these 'new-fangled Yankee boats', and of their good points. There were perks - such as being given a tablet and a half of soap and two semi-used torch batteries, of little value now but then regarded as a much prized gift. Transit through E-boat alley usually resulted in excitement and sleeping fully dressed 'just in case'. Later the ship is adopted by a West Country school, letters are exchanged and some of the crew visit the school. Christmas is celebrated at the buoys. The book ends with the author signing off and *Hampden Z. Coney* loading general cargo for the D-Day beaches.

There are no illustrations but if you are looking for an insight into what it was like on smaller ships during the war I can thoroughly recommend this book. I have seen *Dirty Little Collier* listed on *www.Abebooks.com* and no doubt it can also be found in second-hand book dealers lists.

For the record *Laban Howes* was completed by the Leatham D. Smith Shipbuilding Company, Sturgeon Bay in April 1943. On completion she was chartered to the Ministry of War Transport, later restyled Ministry of Transport, and bought by them in 1947. In April 1949 *Laban Howes* was sold to the Ulster Steamship Co. Ltd. and renamed *Kinsale Head*. They parted with her in 1953 and she held the names *Tela* and *Mariangela B* under the flags of Honduras and Panama before arriving at La Spezia in May 1962 to be broken up.

Abbreviations
A couple of readers have commented that there is no dictionary or similar publication which lists maritime abbreviations and their meanings. Two are used in this article – MMS and KFK. Although they would have to be included, Panamax and Suezmax to quote but two, are well known and understood but do you know of any publication which lists these and any others which feature in maritime journals? If anyone can recommend a suitable publication, or would be interested in compiling such a list with concise explanations, do please let us know. If a decent list was available we could consider publication in Record.

e-Bay
I am sure some of you watch out for interesting items offered on e-Bay. I do and from time to time find something which appeals to me. A couple of weeks back a photograph was offered for sale of the *Elstree Grange* completed in 1916, a bow-on view which I would not normally consider. What made all the difference was that it had been taken at Buenos Aires in July 1937 following a collision with Prince Line's *Southern Prince*. As you can see the damage was considerable. A hefty bid was placed in the hope of securing the picture for use in Record, but someone topped my bid by £1.00, the photo going for the princely sum of £21.00. In view of the interest of a number of our readers in all matters 'Houlder' I feel it is worth reproducing the picture below.

I hope Lesley, the lucky buyer of the photo, will forgive me for taking the liberty of reproducing the photo and if he contacts me I will send him a copy of 'Record' 32 with our thanks and compliments.

Photographs to identify
Overleaf we have a further selection of photographs on which to test your memory, skill and ingenuity. I include memory as it is

Above: *Kinsale Head.* [G. E. P. Brownell/World Ship Society Ltd.]
Right: *Elstree Grange* with considerable bow damage.

always possible you have seen the photo before, named, in some other publication. There are just four but we have tried to include a variety of types as you will note. There is very little to help with these photos – no postmarks or messages to give clues to the place or period. After including a weird and wonderful piece of machinery in 'Record' 31, and having no response I think we will have to stay with ships and ports in the future. , We have had a number of replies concerning photos in 'Record' 31 and earlier issues which have been combined and set out below.

Photo 03/29 *Polykarp*

Tony Pawlyn has very kindly provided further information on the damaged *Polykarp*, pictured in *Record* 29.

The wooden Norwegian barque *Polykarp* (509/1880) left Barry with a cargo of 715 tons of coal for Pernambuco on Sunday 23rd December 1900. On 28th December she was off Kinsale when caught in a severe gale, perhaps reaching hurricane force. Even furled sails were ripped off by the wind, and after running before the gale before some hours it was found the barque was leaking badly. The windmill pump was started, but its fans were ripped off. The remaining pump was soon choked with coal. To make matters worse, the coal cargo shifted and *Polykarp* took a list to port. With ten feet of water in the hold, Captain Rasmussen and his crew of ten prepared for the worst.

However, help came in time. Whilst *Polykarp* was off the Scillies, a Danish steamer launched a boat and took off seven members of the barque's crew, whilst the steam trawler *Sea Hawk* took the *Polykarp* in tow, although not without some difficulty. The trawler dropped her tow off Porthleven where the *Polykarp* anchored on 29th December, whilst the Porthleven lifeboat came out to give any necessary assistance. Next day, the barque was towed into Penzance by the Falmouth tug *Dragon* and the salvage steamer *Greencastle*, and grounded on the hard between the two piers. She remained there for at least a week whilst her coal cargo was unloaded, after which she was moved into the harbour. She was in the condition seen in 'Record' 29, and as well as the damage to her bowsprit and foretopmast, a portion of her port bulwarks had been swept away. The foretopmast has carried away at the doubling, but remains suspended, cap downwards against the back stays. The jib-boom is run in over the galley roof, whilst the bowsprit is canted up and to starboard at an acute angle. Much of the wreckage of her rigging is still on board. Tony points out that, although described as a barque, she was rigged as a barquentine, crossing no yards on the main or mizzen masts. *Polykarp* was repaired in Penzance and returned to service.

Polykarp was not the only victim of this gale. The 'Cornishman' reported that the French barque *Seine* was wrecked at Perranporth on 28th December, the ship *Capricorn* lost near Bude, the iron four-master *Primrose Hill* wrecked near the South Stack, Holyhead, and several local fishing boats lost.

Photo 02/31.

Thanks particularly to Dag Bakka of Bergen, and also Einar O. Onsøien of Hof and Dave Hocquard of Jersey, this wooden coaster has been conclusively identified as *Beco*, not *Deco* as the name on the bow suggested. As Dag says, she has an interesting story.

Cut off from ordinary shipping during the Second World War, there was an upsurge in wooden shipbuilding in Norway, mostly for combined fishing vessel/coasters. The larger vessels were around 90 feet in length, but there were also a number around 120 feet overall, constructed in fir, the last wooden ships built in the country – interestingly, all by South Coast shipyards which had been active in the wooden shipbuilding boom of the 1870s.

In all, 10 wooden coasters of about 120 feet were built between 1941 and 1946. Six were built by Ancas Treskibsbyggeri, Tromoya/Arendal: the *Norfart* in 1942, *Norfisk* in 1942, *Transit* in 1943, *Trollhaug* in 1944, *Randoy* in 1945

and *Peco* in 1946. Three came from Lindstols Skibsbyggeri near Risor: *Freikoll* in 1941, *Breiva* in 1943 and *Norfjell* in 1946. From Hollen Treskibsbyggeri (treskibsbyggeri = wooden shipbuilding yard), Hollen near Kristiansand came *Heroy* in 1946.

Beco was a product of Ancas and quite typical of the design: engine and accommodation were aft, one hold, two hatches, pure motor vessels - not the sort of auxiliaries built in Sweden at the time. The engines were mostly four-cylinder two-stroke, single-acting of Union or Wichmann makes, of 350-400 BHP. Most were employed in the fish trade, and some - including *Beco* - were fitted with refrigerating plants for carrying frozen fish to the UK/Continent. Wooden coasters were by no means rare during the first decades after the war. There were a large number of older vessels around, with scores of converted MMSs and a few German KFKs. *Beco* and her sisters proved quite long-lasting; the last being withdrawn about 1980. The photograph appears to have been taken during the late 1950s, after renaming *Beco*, but before the fitting of radar. The vessel was completed in October 1946, originally as *Peco*, for Skips-A/S Peco (Eugen Pedersen), Bodo. The owners went bankrupt in 1955, after which the vessel was acquired by Kaare Bertnes PR, Bodo and was renamed *Beco*.

'Lloyd's Index' entries from the early 1960s show her still in the fish trade, with frequent voyages from Northern Norway to Grimsby and Hamburg, also from Stornoway to Hamburg and Grimsby to Ventspils.

Beco was sold in January 1966 to North Star Shipping Ltd, Halifax, Nova Scotia for £25,000, and renamed *North Star* under Panama registry. Despite her Canadian ownership, she met her end running aground at Corfu in the Ionian Sea on 8th January 1968, reportedly with a cargo of cigarettes. Although refloated, she was declared a constructive total loss.

Photo 01/31.

It has been suggested that this small passenger/cargo steamer is the *Lafonia* of 1915, owned by Falkland Islands Co. Ltd., London from 1946 to 1950, and formerly the *Perth* of the Dundee, Perth and London Shipping Co. Ltd. However, although there are many similarities, an illustration in Graeme Somner's history of the latter company shows *Lafonia* to have been a more heavily built ship, with a forecastle and bridge deck.

Readers in New Zealand are in no doubt that she is the *Arahura* of the Union Steam Ship Company of New Zealand Ltd. A photograph on page 74 of Ian Farquhar's splendid 'Union Fleet' matches her in every particular. Built by Dennys in 1905, *Arahura* was mainly employed between Wellington, Nelson, Westport and Greymouth and later on the east coast ports of Napier, Gisborne and Auckland. As to the location, John Dawson of New Plymouth thinks it might be Nelson. She appears to be working, having steam around the top of the funnel and the ropes on the after mast look like they are working. The railway wagon on the siding is of a type used in the early days of the Nelson-Glenhope railway.

Sold in 1925 to Anchor Shipping and Foundry Co. Ltd. of Nelson. In 1949 she was sold again and after being laid up and partly dismantled, on 24th January 1952 she was sunk as a practice target by De Havilland Mosquitoes of the Royal New Zealand Air Force.

Thanks to Ian Farquhar of Dunedin, Brent Chambers of Auckland, John Hill of Hexham, Christy MacHale of Liverpool, W.S. Ogilvie of Kilwinning, Barry Parsons of Auckland, Tony Smythe of Rayleigh and Alan Phipps of Droitwich.

A domestic matter

To conclude, a quick word of congratulation to Roy Fenton, one of the partner's in Ships in Focus, who has recently been awarded a PhD. His thesis was about coastal shipping, looking at the change from sail to steam in the UK coastal bulk trades in the latter half of the nineteenth century. Dr Fenton says it won't go to his head: he will still let anyone buy him a beer.

Above: **01/32** There is no indication when or where the photo was taken. The funnel has been tinted with a black top, white band, blue band and red at the bottom.

Right: **02/32** Again no clues as to when or where. The name of the ship may be *Zealander* but it is not clear. The American flag flies at the foremast however the one on the bow is unclear.

Bottom left: **03/32** An early steamer - note the two very thin, tall funnels. On the back of the card is a hand written note 'Loading the *Dubuqoe* at Colon, Panama'. Some men to the left, not shown here, could be in military uniform. Does anyone know anything of the *Dubuqoe* ?

Bottom right: **03/32** What a good photo of a small coaster ! Just a small part of her name is legible, the last four letters '*burn*'. Also where is she ? The pierhead to the left, the church on the horizon above the village and the hill to the right may help bring a result.

INDEX TO RECORD 29 TO 32

Issue numbers are shown in bold

Index of articles

Index of ships

262